TOXIC THINKING

5 SIMPLE WAYS TO TAKE CONTROL OF YOUR THOUGHTS & EMOTIONS

K.C. MYLER

Created with Vellum

CONTENTS

INTRODUCTION

"The only place where your dream becomes impossible is in your own thinking"

— BY ROBERT H. SCHULLER

I have a life-changing suggestion for you. The next time you are out on the street, walk past a stranger and as you pass them, look right in their eyes and say, "You are so stupid!" Then, just carry on walking.

I'm guessing that you find this idea completely shocking, as well you should. "Why would I say such an unkind thing to someone that I don't even know?" Well, *I* don't know why you would want to do that, but I can tell you that you do it every single day...to yourself.

You balk at the idea of saying something so hurtful to someone you'll probably never see again, but you don't think twice about saying even worse things to yourself—the one person you have to live with for the rest of your life.

I do want to be clear here. When I say "you," I include myself in that, because, for a long time, I did this too. I have certainly not been exempt from the vicious circle of toxic thinking, negative self-talk, and the resultant emotional suffering in my life so far. In fact, not that long ago, I was the one devouring resources that would help me out of the trap I had created in my own mind.

I was born in Ireland but moved to Baltimore, Maryland with my family when I was very young. If you are at all familiar with the fiery Irish passion, you'll have a glimpse into how toxic my thinking became. I didn't just berate myself lightly, I overwhelmed myself with insults and negativity. My love for writing, my innate curiosity, and my exploratory nature would lead me to a deeper understanding of what I was doing to myself and my life.

I have returned from a pretty dark place that I had created all on my own. Being intimately familiar with how damaging toxic thinking can be, I began to research. Research is my fallback when I feel completely overwhelmed, and the more I learned about the human mind, the more I started to understand the true nature of the toxic thinking loop. I realized that psychiatry, psychology, and neuroscience had studied these ideas too, and it wasn't long until I felt that there was hope. Finally, I could get myself out of the hole I had been in.

Through the consistent application of the techniques that I will share with you in this book, I was able to beat my self-doubt and elevate my self-esteem. It certainly didn't happen overnight, but after some work, I could feel myself standing up straighter; I finally owned my place in the world, and it felt amazing.

Even though I started to see changes in myself, I still felt the need to learn more, so my study of the elements of toxic thinking continued and the more knowledge I gained, the more empowered I felt to apply these practices in my own life. So now, I feel empowered enough to share this knowledge and these practices and techniques with you.

Writing this book has been yet another turning point in my journey. I am just one person, but I feel that if my research and insights can help bring just one other person out of the dark place that toxic thinking can take you into, then it's all been worth it.

With this book, I want you to gain two things: understanding and empowerment. I want you to truly understand how these negative loops are created, reinforced and how they can be smashed and replaced. I also want you to feel empowered to change the course of your own story as I did mine.

I will address topics like negative self-talk, the creation of habits and unveil the mystery of self-sabotage. I'll also look at your inner critic, how you can control your emotions and thoughts and stop them from taking over your life. I've come across various therapies in my research, and I've found parts that work for me and others that don't. I'll present to you techniques of Cognitive Behavioral Therapy, as well as those of Acceptance and Commitment Therapy theory. I want this book to be accessible and easy for everyone to understand and benefit from, so when I cover these topics, I don't use too much jargon or language that will detract from the meaning.

We are just ordinary people here, you and me, and there are plenty of psychology textbooks out there if that's what you're looking for. This book is a summary of my journey and my findings and takeaways along the way. It is also a guidebook to help you escape from the very same toxic thinking hell that I was caught up in.

More than how toxic thinking develops, I want you to learn how to restructure those thoughts. That, for me at least, is the most important part. We cannot turn back time and undo any damage that has already been done, but we most certainly can learn to unlearn these negative loops.

Self-esteem is a big part of overcoming toxic thinking, and I'll be focusing on this too. Most successful people don't think about what a huge role confidence plays in their success, and even if they do acknowledge it, they definitely won't be able to tell you how to become self-confident. That's a problem because it's a big part of our journey.

In writing this book, I did think it would be nice to see all of my research and the techniques that worked for me in one place, but more than that, I look forward to hearing about your journey and the changes you have been able to create in your life.

The human mind is a powerful place, and we are about to go on a deep dive together to explore the elements of toxic thinking. It will be an interesting, fascinating, and sometimes surprising journey, but I can assure you, it will be one of the most fascinating of your life.

1

A VOICE WITHIN—UNDERSTANDING NEGATIVE SELF-TALK AND THE TOXIC EFFECTS

In this opening chapter, I want to address one of the most powerful parts of the toxic thinking circle: the inner critic. We all have that inner voice that is sometimes helpful in making judgments, but when that voice becomes too loud, it can drown out everything else, become negative, and hamper our quality of life.

I met my inner critic a long time ago, but I only acknowledged her presence when I started to realize how much damage she had done in my life. Before then, I thought about my inner critic in different terms. It was my reasonable side or my logic; sometimes I thought of it as my conscience. The truth is that it was none of those things. My inner critic, although occasionally helpful, was, for the most part, not my friend. When I realized this, I started to look into what this inner dialogue really was and why it was there at all.

The Voice Within

I want to start this section off by making it very clear that your inner voice is not your enemy. Everyone has an internal monologue, and it is something that is constantly happening in our heads. Yet, most of the time, we aren't even aware of it.

This internal monologue, or series of self-generated thoughts, can, for the most part, be quite helpful. It can help us to plan, make decisions, process critical thinking, and self-reflect. We most commonly refer to this internal monologue as self-talk. While we very often hear self-talk mentioned in a negative connotation, this is inaccurate. Self-talk can be positive and negative. It can be neutral too. Since it is also the source of our emotions and moods, we need to understand how this internal monologue can impact us and how we can use it to our benefit.

Distinguishing Between Positive and Negative Self Talk

For example, consider two ad agency employees sitting in a brainstorming session for a new ad campaign. Both employees are at a junior level and working toward proving themselves. The client in question is a massive gain for the agency, and the team that gets to work on this project will be in the limelight. Everyone knows that it's an excellent opportunity to shine.

The meeting, an open session where everyone is encouraged to air their views and ideas, is chaired by the head creative manager. The manager has started sketching out an idea on the whiteboard, and it becomes clear to the two junior employees that something is missing.

One employee, Sam, believes she's identified key criteria about the customer base they are targeting that is being missed in the proposed campaign. She has previously worked on similar campaigns and feels like her views could definitely help. Her internal monologue sounds something like this: "I firmly believe that my ideas can contribute to a successful ad campaign pitch to this client. I would be interested to hear the views of my colleagues and what the more senior members of the team think."

Another employee, Tom, also sees some gaps in the campaign. Although he thinks that he has something valuable to add, he's in two minds about whether he can bring across the ideas in a way that the team and his manager will understand. His internal monologue sounds like this: "I do think that my ideas are interesting, but someone else will probably come up with them anyway. Plus, my manager might think the points are unimportant, and he might be dismissive. It's not worth raising my hand."

Both employees are experiencing some form of internal monologue. Sam's self-talk is more positive, and it's motivating her to share her points with the rest of the group. On the other hand, Tom's self-talk is more negative, and it's convincing him that he should keep his thoughts to himself rather than risk not being taken seriously.

What would happen if, following these two forms of clearly distinct positive and negative self-talk narratives, both employees did share their ideas with the group? How would their form of self-talk impact their perception of the reaction the group and their manager have to their ideas?

Sam, buoyed by positive self-talk, thinks that although some of her points may have been challenged by her colleagues, she learned something new. She also feels that if she does some more research and upgrades her ideas, she could benefit from another similar session.

On the other hand, if Tom had still raised his points, his perception of the outcome would still be colored by the negative self-talk he initially allowed to go on in his head. Despite his ideas being viewed in the very same light that Sam's were, he focuses predominantly on the fact that he didn't receive an overwhelmingly positive response. Even after he leaves the meeting, he continues to obsess over the parts of his ideas that were challenged and thinks that he must have failed to bring them across accurately. As a result, he starts to believe that it is better not to speak up in the future.

Understanding Negative Self-Talk

Just as it's essential to understand that not all self-talk is negative, we should also consider that not all negative self-talk is bad. At times, our inner critic can actually help to keep us motivated. It might remind us that we should not be eating that extra slice of pizza if we are trying to lose weight or that it's probably not a great idea to have that drink for the road.

While occasions such as those mentioned above do occur, negative self-talk can be very destructive for the most part. Negative self-talk can affect our body, mind, and really, our entire lives if we allow it to, but it's not just us that it impacts—it can be toxic for those around us as well.

The average human being experiences between 12,000 and 60,00 thoughts per day (Simone, 2017). About 80% of those thoughts are thought to have a negative connotation, and at least 95% of them are simply repetitive thoughts from the previous day/s. The stories that we tell ourselves on a consistent basis reflect not only our thoughts but also how we are likely to feel and act. Our words and thoughts, therefore, influence the type of reality we create for ourselves. Due to our human tendency to focus more on negative experiences and less on positive experiences, we also tend to learn too much from negative experiences and not nearly enough from positive experiences (Simone, 2017). If negative thoughts start to overwhelm positive thoughts, they can send us into a dangerous downward spiral.

In situations in which we are fearful, negative self-talk can result in a cognitive distortion called 'catastrophizing.' As the name suggests, this is when our negative inner monologue ramps up and turns one small fear into a series of possible catastrophes. An example of this could be a fear of failing if you try a new job role. Let's say, for instance, you've been offered a promotion, but it will take you into a role you have never worked in before, and you are unsure that you have the skills it will take to be successful. Your fear is simple. You're afraid you will fail. The ideal would be to overwhelm that fear with proof of your competency—others have seen your potential and granted the promotion, you have performed well in the past, and when you started your previous roles, you had to learn new skills then, and you did. Unfortunately, if you allow yourself to, instead, be overwhelmed by negative thoughts, you may find that you create a catastrophe out of a failure that has not even occurred yet. Catastrophizing can be identified as a series of "what ifs." It starts with, "what if I fail?" Then, it may lead to, "what if I fail and then I get fired?" Next up is inevitably all the economic and lifestyle problems that will come from that, "what if I don't have an income, lose my house, end up homeless, lose everything that I have, and..." I have no doubt that the over-exaggeration and ridiculous loop that this catastrophic thinking has taken resonates with you in some way. Somehow you have gone from getting a promotion to being homeless in seconds. Of course, that hasn't really happened, but if you continue to allow this negative self-talk on an ongoing basis, you are likely to paralyze your own progress.

Negative self-talk is often also referred to as a cognitive distortion. This word 'distortion' is vital to focus on as it points to the unhelpfulness of this type of self-talk. If something is distorted, that means it is not a reflection of the truth. From this, we can surmise that this consistent, negative internal dialogue occurs due to our cognitively distorted reality to lean toward the most negative of possibilities. If we start to understand that negative self-talk is not a fair representation of the truth, perhaps we can begin to look for the actual truth instead.

Negative self-talk can take different forms. Sometimes it sounds completely reasonable: "I know I'm not good at public speaking, so I'm not going to put myself through this. It's pointless." In other situations, it can sound quite nasty: "I am so dumb. Why can't I just do this right?" It may even masquerade as a realistic summing up of a situation: "I forgot half my speech, clearly that means that I am not good at public speaking." Unfortunately, such seemingly realistic appraisals can quickly dissolve into a fearful over-exaggeration of what this means for your life: "If I can't speak in public, I will never be able to progress in my job. I'll be stuck as a clerk forever."

You may find that the vocabulary your negative self-talk uses sounds suspiciously like a human critic you may have known in the past (or still know).

If your inner dialogue limits your self-belief and prevents you from acknowledging your abilities and fulfilling your full potential, it can be considered negative self-talk. Any thought that reduces your ability to take positive actions in your life, or diminishes your self-confidence, can also be regarded as a negative inner dialogue. This can not only create unnecessary stress in your life, but it can hold you back and limit your growth.

Negative self-talk can become habitual and linked—as all habits are—to certain triggers. You might be driving in traffic and see another driver do something that sets you off, and your immediate thought is that this person has no regard for your safety. If you throw a bit of catastrophizing in there, you may even think they are out to hurt you. Another example could be getting a text from your partner, who is well-known for not being the most expressive in texts. The text very simply reads, "I have something very important to talk to you about when we get home." Your cognitive distortion habit may immediately take you to the point of wondering what you've done wrong. Is your partner upset with you? Have they met someone else? Are they sick? You'll probably just find that your partner saw a great package travel tour and wanted to discuss it with you. Thanks to your negative self-talk habit, though, you may have wasted time and energy worrying about something that was a complete distortion of reality.

All of these thoughts and bits of self-talk add up to a narrative that you tell yourself about your life and the events you experience. Think of your inner voice like the narrator in the audiobook version of your life. While this may sound a little simplistic, it is actually very powerful because our self-talk can shape our reality, as we have already started to discover.

One of the most important parts of understanding what self-talk is is understanding how it is a habit, and, as we well know from recent groundbreaking books around habit forming, habits that are made can be broken and reformed.

Now we understand the nature of the beast, and we know at least some of the consequences that can come from negative self-talk, but this topic warrants a bit more in-depth analysis.

"When you focus on the good, the good gets better."

— ABRAHAM HICKS

2

THE NATURE OF HABITS—ESCAPING THE HAMSTER WHEEL

As we have come to understand thus far, negative self-talk is a habit. Habits also become a vicious circle, and negative self-talk is no different in that respect. You may have already started to understand how toxic negative self-talk can be, but it is certainly crucial for us to delve deeper into this. Once you understand just how detrimental negative self-talk can be, you will be more likely to look out for it. When you can identify it, you can change it.

The Real Consequences of Negative Self Talk

A study published in 2013 indicated that self-blame over negative events and information rumination (the constant running over of scenarios in one's head) increases the risk factor for developing mental health issues (Scott, 2020).

By focusing on negative thoughts, you may decrease your motivation levels, which may lead to increased feelings of helplessness. Consistent negative self-talk has even been linked to the development of depression. People that very often engage in negative inner dialogue have higher levels of stress in their lives. For the most part, this is because their reality is altered, and a space is created in their lives through this negative self-talk, in which they are unable to attain any of the goals they have set for themselves.

When you focus on negative thoughts, you are less likely to see opportunities when they present themselves; you may also find it more challenging to take advantage of these opportunities if you do see them. The high levels of stress that come from negative self-talk are not just from the behaviors themselves but also from your perception of the situation.

Negative self-talk can manifest in a few different ways, and it's important to be able to recognize what it looks like when it comes up in your life:

Self-Limiting Thoughts: With very little proof, you continually tell yourself that you cannot do something, and you end up convincing yourself of your own incapability. For example, you started to believe that you weren't athletically inclined at some stage in your life. Perhaps you didn't do well in gym class at school. You tell yourself that you aren't good at anything sporty or any form of physical activity throughout your life. You've told yourself that for so long that you now believe it, and this self-limiting belief stops you from trying any type of sport or physical activity.

So often, we are unsure of what we are dealing with regarding negative self-talk, so we take it to be the voice of truth. We increasingly rely on it as we consider it to be an honest opinion on our motives, actions, and pursuits of ego.

Perfectionism: You craft negative thought narratives around how "perfect" you need to be in order to be successful. As a result, you start to believe that if any attempt is not 100% perfect in nature, it is a failure. In reality, most successful people are not perfectionists, and none of their attempts at anything were perfect; but they were able to override that desire for perfection. Perfectionist thinking is stressful and, for the most part, pointless because it does not help you get better at anything.

Increased Feelings of Depression: Here, we witness quite a vicious circle. Low levels of serotonin and other biological causes of depression can increase the likelihood of negative self-talk, but your internal critic will, by the same token, increase the depth of your experience of depression. Constant doubt in our abilities and ruminating over negative experiences can leave us exposed to several mental health issues that can progressively worsen over time.

Problematic Relationships: Consistent negative self-talk can wear down our self-esteem and makes us needy and insecure. A negative internal dialogue can also lead to poor communication and a highly critical attitude toward others, which can be very damaging in the long term. Neither of these qualities is beneficial to our interpersonal relationships, whether with friends, romantic partners, or even family members.

One of the most important things that we need to understand about negative self-talk is that it is a great predictor of failure. If you continue to tell yourself that you're going to fail, there is a good chance you will talk yourself into that failure.

On the other side of the coin, a positive internal dialogue is a factor consistently seen in successful people. In one study conducted among athletes (Scott, 2020), when participants were exposed to four different forms of self-talk: motivational, instructional, negative, or positive, almost without fail, those in the group exposed to positive self-talk were most successful.

When we entertain the perception that our self-talk is helpful, it can frequently lead us to engage in negative self-talk. Negative self-talk can lead to us limiting ourselves from interacting socially. We start to focus almost solely on one aspect of our lives and abandon all other ventures and activities. This only serves to worsen our mental state and creates even more self-doubt.

The sad reality of negative self-talk is that no matter how much we achieve, if we allow ourselves to get caught up in believing our internal monologue, then our achievements will never seem good enough. We will constantly feel that the achievements of others are far more substantial or important than our own. Regardless of how many people compliment us on our work, we may still believe that our talent is no greater than anyone else's. Negative self-talk can

cause us to believe that our skills will never be sufficient to compete with everyone else and that we are simply setting ourselves up for rejection.

When we become so significantly critical of ourselves, it can be very easy to become isolated. It is interesting when you are able to break out of this cycle of negative thinking, to go back and read journals and notes you may have made at that time. This often helps to provide a window into just how dysfunctional our thought processes become due to our negative self-talk.

Identifying Negative Self-Talk

To avoid being deeply impacted by negative self-talk, we need to be able to identify it. There are four common forms of self-talk, and it is important for us to be able to distinguish between these types:

Personalizing: This is when you automatically blame yourself for anything bad that has happened. An example of this would be your friend canceling a dinner date because she's had something come up unexpectedly and, instead of believing your friend, you choose to believe that it is actually because she doesn't want to see you. You spend the rest of the evening trying to figure out what you may have done to offend her. A nuance of this type of self-talk is taking responsibility for everything, even things that you have no control over.

Filtering: This is when you dwell only on the negative aspects of a situation or experience, and you filter out anything that could be considered positive or valuable. An example of this could be a working mom who gets called in for a parent-teacher conference. The teacher expresses how well the mom's child is doing in most subjects and how well adjusted and kind the child is. The teacher suggests that she may want to consider extra maths lessons for the child as that does seem to be an area she struggles in. The mom practices filtering self-talk by going home and berating herself for not noticing that her child struggles with math and concludes that she is a bad mother who is not paying enough attention to her child. She has completely filtered out the positive aspects of the conversation, which were actually in the majority, and painted a picture of a pretty successful parent. Instead, she chooses to focus only on what she thinks she has failed at.

Catastrophizing: This is when you automatically anticipate the worst-case scenario being the most likely outcome despite there being little evidence to support this. An example of this is spilling coffee on your shirt on your way to work, and instead of just seeing this as some isolated bad luck, you are sure it is an omen of an even worse day ahead. Catastrophizing can also be a common form of self-talk when it comes to our health. You may have found this even more prevalent during the pandemic when, for instance, you may have developed allergies, and your first thought was that it was something worse.

Polarizing: This is when we see the world through a lens of only good or bad. As a result, we end up chasing an ideal of perfection as we fail to see that there can be a result that has both positive and negative elements. An example of this is having given a fantastic presentation at work, but perhaps you accidentally left out a specific point. Although you received resounding applause and no one in your audience knows that you didn't deliver a point you intended to, you see your presentation in a poor light because it was not exactly how you intended it to be.

Besides these four, there are also other forms of self-talk that are more nuanced. These include:

Mind Reading: This is where you assume that you know what others are thinking without any evidence. Most often, this takes a negative bias. An example of this would be having someone cut you off in traffic and assuming that the person did so intentionally because they think their needs are more important than your own. In reality, you don't know whether that person had any ill-intent at all toward you. They may just have been distracted after having had a really difficult day.

Overgeneralization: This is when you get into the habit of telling yourself that there is no doubt that a negative event is going to repeat itself in the future. An example of this could look like you being reprimanded at work for something that you don't think was your fault. Even though you know that this is likely an isolated event, you may overgeneralize and make yourself believe that such instances will repeat themselves in the future. As a result, you may become hypersensitive whenever events seem to be leading in that direction.

Magnification: This is when we exaggerate our flaws or errors. It is a form of catastrophizing, but it faces inwardly. Hence, instead of recognizing that any difficulty we have or skill we lack can be addressed and improved upon, we convince ourselves that there is no hope of improvement. An example of this might be you stumbling or stammering for a bit in a presentation. Instead of seeing this for what it is—you lost focus for a moment or perhaps didn't prepare well enough—you magnify this by saying that you are incapable of public speaking and should not speak in meetings again for fear of making a fool of yourself.

Minimization: This is the opposite of magnification and involves downplaying our true abilities and being scornful of our strengths. An example of this could be you being offered a promotion into a role at work that requires a very specific skill set. If you allow minimizing self-talk to take hold, you may well talk yourself out of taking the promotion by convincing yourself that the skill set you have is, actually, not as advanced as everything thinks it is.

Emotional reasoning: This involves making decisions based on the emotions we are feeling rather than basing them on our values. A typical example of this is a fear-based decision in which you choose not to stand up for someone in a junior position who is perhaps being unfairly treated. Although your own personal value system tells you that the right thing to do is point out the injustice at play, your fear overrides this, and you do not speak up.

Black and white thinking: This nuance of self-talk is the closest to being polarizing. It is the habit of constantly evaluating situations in extreme categories. This is often turned inward, and you may convince yourself that you cannot be a good person if you have also done something that you are ashamed of. In other words, there can be no middle ground.

Fortune telling: This is the habit of consistently predicting negative outcomes even when there is no evidence to support such an outcome. An example of this would be walking into an exam that you are well prepared for and believing that you will fail because you think something will go wrong. The evidence at hand should lead you to believe that, unless you experience sudden memory loss, your preparation should be enough to ensure a pass in the exam. Still, your fortune-telling self-talk does not allow you to see this as an option.

Labeling: We are pretty familiar with what it looks like to place labels on other people, but we also do this to ourselves through our self-talk. These labels are usually highly inaccurate or very judgemental. An example of this is how we so often call ourselves 'stupid' when we make a simple mistake or label ourselves 'clumsy' because we accidentally broke something.

'Should' statements: This is when we assign a level of certainty to our actions that are unfair and unrealistic. We say that we 'should' or 'should not' have done something when it was always going to be a difficult situation to navigate. This creates false expectations for ourselves, and when we don't meet those expectations, we experience anxiety and frustration.

The four main forms of negative self-talk and their various nuances are the general categories into which our negative internal narratives are placed. The benefit of understanding these various forms is that it helps us to identify these thoughts in ourselves. You may very well have been reading through the list above and found yourself admitting that you've been guilty of one or more of these types of negative self-talk before. For the most part, we have all experienced most of these forms at some time or another. In isolation, they are not particularly damaging, but when they become repetitive, and our brains accept these thought patterns as helpful, they become a problem.

As with any challenge in our lives, once we can recognize the problem, we can start to move toward fixing it. In addition, these labels of negative self-talk tend to overlap with cognitive distortions, and we end up believing things about ourselves and the world that are not true.

More About Mindfulness

Mindfulness is a concept we address quite often in this book, and I think it bears a deeper dive so that we truly understand its nature.

Mindfulness is simply the idea that you are fully attending to what is happening, the space you are moving through, and what you are doing. The idea might seem trivial on its own until you acknowledge that we so often veer from what is happening in the here and now. Our mind starts to roam, we lose touch with what is happening in our body, and very soon, we are completely engrossed in obsessive thoughts about something that happened in the past, or we find ourselves stressing about something that hasn't even happened yet. This is a breeding ground for anxiety and wasted energy.

Mindfulness is the natural human ability—yes, one you are born with—to be fully present, completely aware of where we are and what we are doing instead of being reactive or becoming overwhelmed by what is happening around us. Mindfulness is a quality that every human being already has—it is not something you have to conjure up magically, you just have to learn how to access it.

While mindfulness is already within us, it can also be cultivated through proven techniques. Here are some examples:

- Walking, seated, moving, and standing meditation.
- Short pauses we consciously insert into our everyday life.
- Assimilating meditation practice with other activities, such as sport or yoga.

When we are mindful, we reduce stress, improve performance, gain insight and awareness by observing our minds, and increase our attention toward the well-being of others. Mindfulness is not exotic or obscure. It is familiar to us because it is what we already do and how we already are. It takes many shapes and goes by many names. We already possess the capacity to be present, and it doesn't mean that we have to change who we are. We can, however, cultivate these innate qualities with simple practices that are scientifically proven to benefit us, our loved ones, our friends, neighbors, our colleagues, and the organizations and institutions we take part in.

Mindfulness does not ask you to change who you are. For the most part, at least in my experience, solutions that ask us to change who we are, or become something we are not, fail us over and over again. Mindfulness recognizes and cultivates the best parts of who we are as people. It has the potential to become a transformative social phenomenon because anyone can do it. The practice of mindfulness cultivates universal human qualities and does not require anyone to change their belief system. Everyone can benefit, and it is easy to learn.

Mindfulness is more than just a practice. It brings awareness and caring into everything we do, and it eliminates unnecessary stress. Even a little bit of mindfulness makes our lives a lot better.

Both science and experience demonstrate the positive benefits of mindfulness for our happiness, health, work, and relationships. Mindfulness also sparks innovation. As we deal with our world's increasing uncertainty and complexity, mindfulness can lead us to resilient, effective, low-cost responses to seemingly complex problems.

The Science Behind Mindfulness

In the last few decades, public interest in mindfulness has accelerated. In parallel to this interest, and perhaps feeding it, has been the growing popular acceptance from the scientific community. Randomized controlled trials are the gold standard for clinical study, and the number of these trials involving mindfulness has jumped from one in the period between 1995 to 1997 to 11 in the period between 2004 to 2006, and then exploded with a prodigious 216 in the period between 2013 and 2015 (Powell, 2018).

Studies have shown an impressive range of both mental and physical benefits that mindfulness has for varying health conditions, including fibromyalgia, irritable bowel syndrome, anxiety, psoriasis, depression, and post-traumatic stress disorder (Powell, 2018).

Much of the research uses functional magnetic resonance imaging (fMRI), which takes snapshots of the brain and records brain activity that occurs during the scan. A study conducted in 2012 shows that the positive changes in brain activity seen during the conscious mindfulness practice remained consistent in subjects even when they were not specifically focusing on being mindful. Researchers took before-and-after scans of people who learned to practice mindfulness over a period of two months. The people were scanned not when they were actively practicing mindfulness but rather while they were performing normal everyday tasks. The scans still showed changes in the subjects' brain activation patterns from the start to the end of the study. This was the first time such a change had been detected in a part of the brain called the amygdala (Powell, 2018). The amygdala is a collection of cells located near the base of the brain. There are two of these, one in each hemisphere of our brains. This is where emotions are remembered, given meaning, and attached to associations and responses to them. The amygdala is part of the brain's limbic system, and it is key to how you process strong emotions like pleasure and fear.

Exercise: Countering Negative Self-Talk

So now that you know what the four main forms of negative-self talk are, how can we go about stopping them from taking over our internal monologue and impacting our life?

In this exercise, you will be guided to recognize and use simple methods to counter the four main types of negative self-talk. Mindfulness and self-awareness are vital here, as you will need to spend time analyzing your own internal monologue in order to identify these forms of negative self-talk. It will also take some analysis to categorize the self-talk you're experiencing correctly.

So take your time and be patient with yourself.

As a reminder, the four types of negative self-talk we are working toward countering are:

1. Personalizing
2. Filtering
3. Catastrophizing
4. Polarizing

1. Combat Personalizing Negative Self-Talk by Zooming Out and Questioning

Suppose you have identified self-talk in which you are placing the blame or responsibility for something on yourself without any evidence. In that case, you will want to use a "zooming out and questioning technique" to start countering this.

For example, perhaps you are part of a group chat to which you send a text, and you find that everyone is taking an unusually long amount of time to reply. If you experience personalizing negative self-talk around this, you may think that the group members are angry with you for some reason or find you boring. The truth, of course, is that perhaps everyone is just busy, and they'll reply when they have time to.

The first part of this exercise is to test the reality of your self-talk. Ask yourself:

- **What evidence exists to support this thought?** Do you know what each of the group members is doing at that moment? Have you done anything to anger your friends?
- **Is this thought my interpretation of the situation, or is it based on fact?** If I told someone else that this was the case, would they agree?

When you have answered these questions, try to think of a different explanation that could go against this personalizing negative thought.

If you find yourself up against a personalizing negative self-talk event, try to see the situation from a different perspective. Consider that the group members could just be busy, or perhaps they aren't in an area with mobile service and haven't even seen your text yet. Both of these reasons are far more realistic than thinking that their non-response is a personal attack on you.

2. Combat Filtering Negative Self-Talk by Journaling Positivity

When you find yourself magnifying the negative parts of a situation and all but ignoring the positive aspects in your self-talk, you are practicing filtering. This is probably one of the most common forms of negative self-talk, especially when you are trying to improve yourself in some way. If you are working on eating healthier, saving money, or creating an exercise habit, it may be easy to allow filtering to sabotage your attempts. If you plan to exercise three times per week, for instance, and only manage two days in the week, filtering may cause you to focus on the one day you missed, and you could start to believe that you may as well not bother because you've already messed up so early in your mission. In reality, you are filtering out the positive parts of this experience and ignoring how much you have achieved. You have gone from being a couch potato to exercising twice in one week—that's pretty awesome! The fact that you missed one day is negligible.

Journaling around the positive aspects of your life and achievements can help to counter filtering. If you are able to do this on a regular basis, it not only builds up a pretty decent guidance document to prove to your inner voice that the negative aspect is not the only part that matters, but the more you encourage your brain to focus on finding the positive in situations, the more likely you will be to automatically see these positive aspects in future.

3. Combat Catastrophizing Negative Self-Talk by Putting Things into Perspective

When you catastrophize, you'll find yourself assuming the absolute worst-case scenario whenever anything vaguely negative happens. Let's say, for instance, that you pull your car out onto the main road that you take to work and find that it is busier than usual. You immediately think that you will be stuck in bumper-to-bumper traffic and be very late for work. You may even go so far as to believe that your boss will be so angry with you for being late that you'll be fired on the spot.

When you find your inner monologue leading you to a worst-case scenario, take a step back and try to put things into perspective. Ask yourself how likely it is that, just because this road is busier than usual, you will find yourself stuck in bumper-to-bumper traffic. Has this happened many times before? What is the likelihood that you really will be stuck for so long that you'll be significantly late for work? Even if you are late, is it realistic to believe that you will get fired for it?

When you view things from a different perspective, it is easier to consider that perhaps there are more realistic and less drastic outcomes to the event you are facing. It also empowers you to acknowledge that, really, no matter what the outcome, you will be able to overcome it.

4. Combat Polarizing with Self-Love and Kindness

When you experience polarizing, you find yourself unable to accept that there is a middle ground and that things are not always black or white. This often happens when we hold ourselves to an unrealistically high standard or when we are on a mission to self-improve in some way. Making one mistake in an otherwise excellent presentation, for instance, does not make you a poor public speaker. Taking one night out to spoil yourself while dieting does not make you a loser.

The only way to get around this polarizing negative self-talk is to accept that you are a human being who is doing your very best in life. It is also necessary to get to a place where you believe that you are worthy of love and kindness no matter how successful you are in your endeavors. While this can be a more extensive conversation than just self-talk and have far deeper roots, it is the essence of defeating polarizing self-talk. By treating yourself with kindness and accepting your humanity and fallibility, you may find yourself being more successful than ever.

Even though it is important to stay fixed to a goal and work hard to get there, there are times when we need to meet our needs as human beings, and often, if we don't do that, we will struggle to attain our goals. So there has to be a middle ground in our lives. Exercise is important, but so is rest. Hard work on a project is vital to success, but your brain needs time to recharge and recover so that you can put your best work in.

The irony of polarizing negative self-talk is that it can take us further away from achieving our goals rather than closer to them. The more we allow this internal monologue to convince us that we are lazy, losers, failures, and all the other negative labels we assert through polarization, the more we hack away at our self-esteem, which is vital to achieving anything.

Try starting your day with positive affirmations, but pick ones that are really personal to you and will help to counter your negative self-talk. Once you've practiced a bit of self-awareness and mindfulness, you will understand your most common negative self-talk phrases, and you can then develop positive affirmations to counter these.

For example, if you commonly find your inner voice telling you that you cannot cope or that you are unable to do something, choose to start your day with a positive affirmation such as: "You've got this!" or "You can do this!"

Some people feel that positive affirmations are unrealistic, but I am not asking you to disregard the reality of a situation. Instead, be realistic, but in a positive light.

Build Habits

After you have worked on these exercises individually and feel that you have a good grasp of them, the best route to permanent change is developing habits that consistently support the countering of the four main types of negative self-talk. Positivity journaling, in particular, is a great habit to develop for reflection as it helps to encourage questioning of negative thoughts and putting things into perspective for a more realistic understanding of the situation.

Habits are built through repetition and reward. The reward from practicing these exercises is reduced anxiety and increased self-esteem. When you start to experience these benefits regularly, you will find yourself far more likely to build habits in these exercises.

Understanding the nature of negative self-talk is vital to overcoming it. Catching yourself in the act is also a significant part of starting to change the tide; you cannot fix what you can't see. I recommend that you practice this exercise as often as possible to attempt to make it a habit in your life. Once you have mastered this, we can move on to the next stage of the process.

"You are what you do, not what you say you'll do."

— C.G. JUNG

3

SELF-SABOTAGE—HOW YOUR OWN EMOTIONS CAN BE DESTRUCTIVE

A major part of conquering negative self-talk is understanding its origins. This can be a little trickier than it sounds, as anything related to the human mind is never simple. By establishing the common sources of negative thoughts, you can start to move toward eliminating them almost completely.

Negative self-talk is self-sabotage. These thoughts are self-generating and feed into emotions that we choose to take forward into our lives. This is why it is essential to understand where this unhelpful internal monologue stems from and nip it in the bud.

Self-Talk—The Voice of Reason

There is significant evidence to point to the origins of self-talk deriving from the early stages of speech and communication skill development in children. Considering the nature of self-talk and the context of our discussion here, it may seem strange to consider that this often negative force in humans could possibly emanate in the innocence of children.

If we think about how children learn to talk, though, and how they practice a language when they are very young, the idea no longer seems so alien. When a child is learning to communicate verbally, they will often talk to themselves, quite happily, for hours on end. For the child, it is an opportunity to practice sounds and words, and it is also the very beginning of them learning how to express emotions verbally.

Psychologists have referred to this type of communication, which is usually displayed by children between the ages of two and seven, as private speech. The communication is not directed at anyone in particular, and children use private speech for self-regulation and self-guidance.

Private speech is believed to aid in developing literacy skills in the early stages of a child's life and can help increase the success of a child's task performance and how easy they find it to achieve goals (Wikipedia Contributors, 2019).

Private speech is prevalent in all mammals, and we can see this in chimpanzees that have been taught sign language. Young chimps have been observed to self-sign when they are performing day-to-day tasks.

This early form of verbal communication which is already aimed at self-regulation, self-guidance, and planning, continues well into the elementary school years of a child. The more they start to socially engage with other children and opportunities for private speech become fewer, this will eventually develop into inner speech. Theoretically, this turning of private speech inward is believed to give rise to both positive and negative self-talk. It becomes an internal critic that we can turn to for guidance around our actions, rumination about our behavior, or assistance in planning the execution of tasks.

When the Past Takes Over

Another theory on the development of our internal monologue is that it emerges as a result of how we were spoken to as children by our parents or other primary caregivers. Many researchers have proposed that our self-talk will often resemble the manner in which we were spoken to during our childhood (Norris, 2018).

During development, children will absorb the guidance they receive from their parents and caregivers so that it can be referred back to in future situations. When a child finds themselves in a similar situation in the future, they can use this guidance they previously received to find their way through the situation at hand. In this way, absorbed guidance from parents is similar to a child's own private speech. Both help to give the child a road map for the future. As we grow and mature, this inner voice may start to spiral out of control depending on the type of experience we have with other people and how we handle stressful situations.

I must say that this particular theory resonates with me, and I think it will with many people. I think that the guidance I received as a child has influenced my inner voice. Simple pieces of advice like, "Don't stay up late," "Make sure you finish your homework," or "Don't talk to strangers" have stuck with me and remain a part of my self-talk to this day.

As children, when we internalize neutral guidance dialogues along with negative experiences, it can strengthen our inner critic or negative self-talk, and we may constantly find ourselves at odds in every situation and thinking negatively about many different scenarios.

While positive and negative self-talk exists in every person, it becomes truly problematic in our lives when we get into a habit of repetition.

Unhelpful Habits Around Self-Talk

Just as constant negative self-talk can lead to self-doubt and isolation, the next part of this vicious circle is how we come to rely on this inner voice. I found this to be a significant part of my experience with negative self-talk. I became so used to being guided by this negative internal monologue that it became a guiding voice for me. I was, perhaps, so convinced that this self-talk was helpful to me that I believed it was important for me to listen to it and consult with it whenever I was unsure about something. While this sounds like a whole process that you would be aware of, it really isn't. Unless you practice self-awareness and mindfulness, you may not know that you are using this consultation process with your inner critic.

Now, this is not just my experience, it is backed up by science. Habitual negative thinking can develop physical neural paths in your brain through a process called neuroplasticity. The more we repeat this process, the deeper the habit becomes ingrained in our lives.

The concept of neuroplasticity is simply explained by saying that the brain is not set in its existing neural pathways. Neural pathways are developed when we learn new skills and develop new habits. At one time, scientists believed that these pathways became fixed at a certain age in adulthood, but we now know that habits and skills can be learned and developed throughout our lifetime. Neuroplasticity can be both a positive and negative thing as we see in the development of negative thinking habits.

Neural pathways are formed by repetition and reward, and your brain will always choose the path of least resistance to perform any action. So if you have continually "taught" your brain that a specific way of thinking is the best course of action, it will build and strengthen the neural pathways that support that way of thinking. Suppose you allow yourself to feel extreme anxiety about the smallest of problems continuously. In that case, your brain will start recognizing this as the best course of action, and, as a result, the neural pathway to anxiety will be forged and strengthened. This same concept applies to all of the forms of negative self-talk we discussed in the previous chapter. If you tend toward either one of these types of negative thinking and repeat that pattern regularly, your brain will reinforce that.

For me, this would become apparent in my complete aversion to constructive criticism. Firstly, I found it very difficult to differentiate between constructive criticism and criticism that could not be helpful. I felt that it was all the same, and it all meant that I was a failure, for the most part. My complete aversion to any type of criticism meant that I preempted this with my own negative self-talk. I simply believed that I was not competent to achieve any of the goals I had set for myself, and this belief, I thought, protected me from criticism. If I didn't try anything, then no one could criticize me for it, right? I don't have to tell you that this was even less fulfilling than experiencing occasional constructive criticism.

Addicted to Negative Self-Talk?

I've always wondered why it is so easy to slip into negative thought patterns, but such an effort needs to be made to switch those patterns to positive ones. In an article in *Psychology Today*, Nancy Colier, a psychotherapist, and author of the book *Can't Stop Thinking,* proposes a reason that resonates with me.

As I've already discussed earlier in this book, the human mind focuses on the negative from an evolutionary perspective.

Although this evolved skill no longer protects us from saber tooth tigers and starvation, it remains an embedded part of our psyche. The main difference now is that our lives are so flooded with incoming information and experiences that we have a lot more to think negatively about. In her article, Colier suggests that our compulsive need to cling to the things that cause us pain and ruminate over what we see as our failures comes as a result of our desire to see a different outcome somehow.

Each time we return to thoughts of a negative experience, we hope that we will be able to rescript it into a different and more positive reality. We feel that by immersing ourselves in these negative thoughts and painful feelings, we will perhaps suddenly see them in a completely different light. Colier says that the paradox is that we hold onto our pain to try and find a way to let it go.

By turning an experience into a series of repetitive thoughts, we also avoid feeling the emotions that come with that negative experience. If we can just have repetitive thoughts about it, then we don't actually have to feel it. Our brains turn this into a habit:

1. Experience something negative
2. Push the feelings down
3. Experience only negative thoughts and rumination as a way of avoiding the emotions

The irony, of course, is that the more we push these feelings down and use negative thoughts to attempt to change the situation, the more we stay in that negative space. By continually entertaining negative thoughts about an event, we believe that we are taking care of ourselves. We think that this process helps us to validate our pain and acknowledge that we were wronged. That negative validation becomes our reward for having experienced this pain.

We know that habits form when three criteria are present:

1. Trigger
2. Routine
3. Reward

Therefore, when we entertain this process of negative thinking, the trigger is any event that causes the negative thinking loop to start. The routine is the thought loop itself, and the reward is the feeling of validation for our pain. These three criteria result in negative thinking becoming a habit and, to some degree, an addiction.

The other side of this coin is that, as human beings, we are also deeply attached to our pain—we believe it forms part of our identity. Our pain is a component of our personal narrative, and as such, deep down, we believe that holding onto it and revisiting it is necessary for us to retain our identity.

7 Trigger Habits That Can Cause Negative Self-Talk

Just as negative self-talk itself can become habitual, it can also be triggered by other unhelpful habits in our life. By identifying the habits that trigger your negative self-talk, you can stop the process from beginning at all, which is preferable to attempting to avoid it once you are already in the loop. The following are seven habits that are common in many of our lives and are known to cause negative self-talk:

1. Failure to address relationship problems
2. Not taking care of your physical health
3. Isolating yourself too frequently
4. Not asking for help
5. Not setting aside time for self-care
6. Attempting to deny that you experience negative self-talk
7. Spending too much time around negative people

If I think about the aversion that I had to criticism, this would cause me to isolate myself because I figured the less interaction I had with others, the less likely I would be to encounter criticism. Unfortunately, the more I was alone with my own thoughts and without the input of others, I found my negative self-talk completely taking over my internal narrative.

Poor health habits are probably one of the most common triggers for negative self-talk, especially if these habits are linked to our physical appearance. If we are unhappy with how we look and we know that changing some of our health habits could help, a failure to do so can become a major source of negative self-talk. Something that I found helpful was not trying to fix everything at once. If you are a little overweight, don't eat well, live a pretty sedentary lifestyle, or smoke, trying to fix all of these habits in one go is going to set you up for failure and a whole lot of negative self-talk. You can divide up these tasks in one of two ways—either pick the one that has the greatest impact on your health, which in this case would be smoking, or choose the one that will be easiest to fix, such as exercise if you just start taking your dog on longer walks, for instance.

I can also say for sure that not asking for help is a major negative self-talk trigger for many people I know and me. The irony is that when I don't ask for help, I still find my inner voice complaining about how I have to do everything myself. There can be many more significant reasons that you don't ask for help. For me, it had a lot to do with how I grew up and the fact that I had to be very self-sufficient. That made it hard for me to ask for help as an adult, as, deep down, I believed that I could not rely on anyone else. It took a long time for me to work through that, but when I did, I found my rate of negative self-talk reducing tremendously.

How to Start Turning the Tide

Now that we are starting to understand where negative self-talk comes from, we need to consider strategies for overcoming toxic thinking. In my experience, there are three major steps to this, they are:

- Silencing the mind
- Detaching yourself
- Transforming the negativity

In the next chapter, we will delve more deeply into these three steps. Before we get into that, though, let's put what we've learned into action.

Exercise: Challenging Our Negative Thoughts

How do we go about challenging these negative thought patterns? Well, the first stage of your exercise is to catch yourself doing it. This takes a good amount of mindfulness, self-awareness, and practice, but it is possible to achieve.

In this exercise, I want to be clear that we are not trying to stop these thoughts from appearing in our heads. That would be a futile exercise as you will never stop yourself from having negative thoughts. The key to this exercise is to learn to automatically challenge them, rather than allow them to take root.

You already know what type of thoughts and self-talk you are looking for, and you may have already been able to identify which types are more common for you.

The next step is to distance yourself from this thought. Try to see it as a separate part of you and consider it with a zoomed-out perspective. Consider how biases and past experiences might be coloring your thoughts. Is this really what you believe, or is it a product of something else? When you are challenging your thoughts, do so with kindness. It is no good using your critical inner voice to try and combat itself. Instead, you need to approach this exercise as though you were a kind, old friend and consider how such a person might treat you. Essentially, you are looking to control your mind rather than having it control you, and in order to do so, you need to practice kind mindfulness.

Try to put your thoughts into two categories: is it helpful or harmful? Be aware that negative thoughts might not present themselves as harmful upfront, but if you do a bit of thinking about where that thought may lead you, its negativity becomes clear.

How would you feel if you had a tiny person sitting on your shoulder telling you what to think? That would be annoying, wouldn't it? You would also probably wonder what gives that person the right to tell you what to think. With that idea in mind, consider that your negative thought loops are doing exactly the same thing. Instead of allowing you to make up your own mind about a situation and how you feel about it, toxic thinking takes that choice away from you. This exercise is all about making that choice again.

You do not have to be controlled and driven by negative thoughts. You *do* have the right and the ability to choose what you think and which thoughts you want to pay attention to. You just have to exercise that right.

After identifying a thought and categorizing it as helpful or harmful, your next step is to decide what you want to think. Perhaps you've just had a thought that something you did was foolish. Is that thought helpful or harmful? Clearly, it's harmful because constantly telling yourself that you are stupid will do nothing to improve your self-esteem. Instead, challenge that thought. Was it really a case of stupidity, or did I just not have all the information I needed at the time to make a better decision? Does this mistake have any reflection on my IQ? Then, decide how you would prefer to frame this and do so with kindness. What can you learn from this experience about the way you make decisions?

Once you have decided what you believe about the situation, use that frame of guidance and move forward by holding onto that rather than the negative false belief that was your initial reaction. This takes practice, and it is by no means a one-off exercise. In order to truly see benefit from this, you will need to be willing to regularly challenge your thoughts and choose to move forward with your new resolutions rather than with the toxic thinking you previously lived with.

"Worrying does not take away tomorrow's troubles, it takes away today's peace."

— RANDY ARMSTRONG

4

SILENCING THE INNER CRITIC—5 SIMPLE STEPS TO CONTROLLING THOUGHTS AND EMOTIONS

In this chapter, we will start to approach the tackling of toxic thinking. As I have previously expressed, this whole journey started for me when I found myself trapped in a rabbit hole of toxic thinking. At the time, it would be a simple piece of advice from a friend that would set me on the path to recovery. In turn, I hope to share this same advice and more with you so that you too, can begin the journey out of that rabbit hole.

I will be sharing five simple tips with you on how to start this journey of recovery, as well as a bonus exercise to help you analyze and counter your toxic thinking habit.

The Advice That Changed my Life

One of the most important things that I learned through my journey out of toxic thinking is that talking about what is going on in your head is absolutely vital. When you allow your thoughts to sit in your head and you don't work through them, they do far more damage. So often, verbalizing what you are thinking makes all the difference in being able to see a new perspective.

When I was at the most difficult stage of my toxic thinking loop, my thoughts spiraled out of control. I had decided to try Cognitive Behavioral Therapy (CBT) as a last-ditch effort to reclaim my life. Thankfully, I had a friend who worked as a therapist in this field, and he shared the most amazing five-minute, three-column technique to help me get started. There will be a practice exercise at the end of this chapter.

Another take on speaking about what is on your mind is to use this scenario to frame your own response to your thoughts. By picturing yourself as the person giving advice, you will be far more likely to address your thoughts and self-talk kindly, rather than reprimanding yourself, which is unhelpful.

By framing the challenging of my thoughts in the manner of kind advice from an old friend, I was able to see how absurdly critical I was to myself. If I talked to a friend and gave them advice, I would never speak to them the way I was talking to myself. So why was it acceptable when the narrative was internal? By being so overly critical and engaging in toxic thinking patterns, I was closing my brain off to the things that I wanted to hear, and instead, I was focusing on all the negative stuff.

Baby Steps to Silence Your Inner Critic

After pushing myself to open up to more people about my thoughts, analyzing my thought patterns, practicing mindful awareness around my self-criticism, and seeking professional therapeutic assistance, I put together a five-step program that I would implement to beat my inner critic.

These are my five steps to silencing the critic:

1. Meditate to practice mindfulness
2. Turn your inner critic into a silly character
3. Stop comparing yourself to other people
4. Practice compassion toward yourself
5. Start self-gratitude journaling

Meditate To Practice Mindfulness

> *"Until you make the unconscious conscious, it will direct your life and you will call it fate."*
>
> — CARL JUNG

I've said it before, and it certainly warrants saying again: you will never overcome your negative thought loops if you are not aware of them. Awareness and mindfulness are always going to be the first steps to silencing your inner critic.

The meditation practice helps us raise awareness of our inner voice by revealing our subconscious thoughts and feelings. By practicing meditation regularly, you will also become more mindful, which will give you the ability to recognize your thoughts before you engage with them. Essentially, you become the observer of your thoughts rather than the one experiencing them. This enables you to consciously choose which thoughts you want to give your energy to rather than allowing each and every thought to automatically demand your attention and energy.

Through our analysis thus far, we have determined that negative self-talk is not made up of factual information for the most part. It is simply a series of ideas that you have chosen to empower, and, as such, they have become a habitual part of your thinking.

Have you ever heard the phrase, "Energy flows where attention goes?" It's often used in productivity circles, and it means that you should pay attention to the things that you want to grow. This concept is applicable in our thought processes, too, and the thoughts you pay attention to will inevitably determine the type of emotions you feel.

By becoming observers of our thoughts through mindfulness and meditation, we can choose which thoughts we wish to pay attention to and simultaneously decide how we want to experience these thoughts emotionally.

Turn Your Inner Critic into a Silly Character

The best way to take the power away from your inner critic is to picture them as a funny character—one that cannot possibly be taken seriously. One of the reasons we take our negative self-talk so seriously is that we assume it must come from some wise part of us deep inside. Of course, we know that this is not true, and picturing your negative self-talk coming from some ridiculous-looking character, makes it easier not to take the narrative to heart.

You can picture a character from a cartoon or movie, but you need to be able to visualize that character and hear their voice for this to work. Then, every time some negative self-talk arises, picture it coming from that character and ask yourself how seriously you should be taking the idea.

Stop Comparing Yourself to Other People

Today, especially with social media being such a popular place for us to advertise our achievements, it is really easy for us to find ourselves comparing our situations and lives to those of others around us. Almost inevitably, no matter how deep your competitive streak runs, you will compare yourself to other people, and the negative self-talk will begin.

I don't have to tell you that no one's life is perfect. No matter how wonderful someone's life looks on social media or how confident and assured a coworker comes across in meetings, they too have their difficulties and challenges. That said, their successes, achievements, challenges, and problems have no bearing on your life. Everyone else has walked a very different path than you, and it stands to reason that they will be in a different place right now than you are.

Comparing yourself to other people, especially when it makes you feel inferior, is not helpful at all. In fact, it's a complete waste of time and energy. If you want to accomplish everything that you set your mind to, make sure that you are using your energy on yourself and not on worrying about other people's journeys.

The only comparison that is helpful is when you compare yourself to who you were the day before. That is a comparison that, when done kindly, helps you to grow.

We can combine this step and the previous one to good measure. Whenever you catch yourself comparing your life, skills, or experiences to anyone else, pretend that your looney inner voice character is saying these things to you. You will soon find yourself shrugging off the comparison as ridiculous.

Practice Compassion Toward Yourself

If you want to stop negative self-talk from taking over your life, you have to accept that every human being, including you, is imperfect. Each individual's beauty lies in their uniqueness, and when you can embrace this as a positive thing, you will be able to move past self-judgment with compassion.

In this step, we go back to the idea of treating ourselves the same way we would an old friend or beloved family member. If such a person approached you with ideas about their failures and weaknesses, there is no way that you would affirm their feelings of insecurity. You would do everything in your power to make them see themselves in the positive light that you do. You would highlight all of their strengths and amazing abilities —all of the reasons you love them. So why would you do anything less for yourself? You, after all, are the sole person that you have to spend the rest of your life with. Your relationship with yourself is the most important you will ever have, so why not nurture it with compassion and kindness rather than destroying it with unfair criticism and bitterness?

The more you give power and energy to being compassionate with yourself, the less energy and power your inner critic will have to destroy your self-confidence. Criticism loses its impact when compassion is present, so being kind to and accepting of yourself is a powerful way to fight negative self-talk.

Start Self-Gratitude Journaling

This is not the first time I've advocated for self-gratitude journaling in this book, and that's because I have found it to be a powerful tool against toxic thinking. While it is great to express gratitude for things that have happened to you during your day and the actions of others that made your life better, the real benefit comes from expressing gratitude for the things we have done, felt, and achieved as individuals.

These do not need to be grand achievements or major successes. Something as simple as eating a healthy breakfast and taking the stairs rather than the elevator is a great point to include in your self-gratitude journal. The key is to work your way through your day from beginning to end and pick out every single thing that you are grateful for. Some days you will have a whole page full, and other days, you may just have one item. The key is that you will start to look for these moments in your day and become far more aware of them; this improves your overall experience of your day-to-day life.

The other great thing that comes from daily self-gratitude journaling is how you feel when you look back on a week's or month's worth of gratitude entries. It's pretty difficult to be down on yourself when you look back at multiple pages containing memories of what you've achieved and succeeded at.

Building Mental Strength

Mental strength and resilience play a significant role in combating negative self-talk. This is because the stronger you are from a mental perspective, the more likely you are to bounce back from negative events, thoughts, and emotions.

Even if you would currently rate your mental strength on a relatively low level, don't despair—just like physical muscles, your mental and emotional muscles can also be built up.

Mental strength starts when you develop the ability to observe what is passing through your mind without allowing it to affect you personally. This is followed up by the ability to create positive thoughts about the situation you find yourself in.

Mental strength can be built by focusing on the following five areas (Ribeiro, 2019):

1. Positive thinking
2. Control of anxiety
3. Visualization
4. Setting of goals
5. Control of attention

In general, mentally strong people are higher achievers and are more content than those that are very sensitive. Mental strength can be measured by the 4 Cs: Control, Commitment, Challenge, and Confidence (Ribeiro, 2019).

Control

This is the degree to which you feel that you are in control of your life, including your sense of purpose and emotions. The control component of mental strength is essentially your self-esteem. If you are high on the control scale, then you have a good sense of self and feel comfortable in your own skin.

In order to increase control over your thoughts, and therefore your life, you need to be able to control your emotions and be less distracted by the feelings of other people. If your ability to control your thoughts is low, you may feel like you have no influence or control over events that happen to you (Ribeiro, 2019). Instead of being proactive about a situation, you are, instead, reactive. When you respond this way, you are far more likely to experience negative thought patterns, which is why working on this area of mental strength is so vital for ceasing the loop of toxic thinking.

Commitment

The commitment component of mental strength is the depth of your reliability and personal focus. If you are high on the commitment scale, you can effectively set goals and be consistent about achieving them without allowing anything to distract you. If you have a high commitment level, you are good at establishing healthy habits and routines that help you cultivate success.

If you are low on the commitment scale where your mental strength is concerned, it indicates that you might find it challenging to set and prioritize your goals. You may also find it hard to adapt to new routines or habits that are indicative of success. Finally, you may be easily distracted by competing priorities or other people.

When combined, the control and commitment components of mental strength represent your mental and emotional resilience. This is because your ability to bounce back from challenges in life requires a sense of feeling that you are in control and that you can make changes successfully. Resilience also means that you need to focus and set up habits and goals that will get you back on your desired path (Ribeiro, 2019).

As it relates to negative thinking, if you have a high level of commitment, you will find yourself less distracted by negative self-talk and more likely to stay focused on the task at hand despite what your inner critic is trying to convince you of.

Challenge

This component of mental strength measures how driven and adaptable you are. Suppose you rank high on the challenge scale. In that case, it means that you are internally driven to achieve your personal best and that you see adversity, challenges, and change more as opportunities rather than difficulties. You are also likely to be agile and flexible. If you are low on the challenge scale, it means that you feel that change is threatening, and you may avoid new or challenging situations that take you out of your comfort zone because you are afraid of failing (Ribeiro, 2019).

Situations in which we experience change, or that take us outside of our comfort zone are fertile grounds for negative thought loops. If you can embrace change and look forward to new opportunities, you are far less likely to experience negative self-talk around such situations.

Confidence

Your confidence level as it relates to mental strength is the extent to which you believe you are capable and able to be productive. It also represents your belief in yourself and your belief in your ability to influence others. If you are high on the confidence scale, you can successfully complete tasks and take setbacks in your stride and maintain your routine. If you are low on the confidence scale, it means that challenges easily disrupt you, and you do not believe in your own capability or that you have influence over other people.

When combined, the challenge and confidence scales represent the confidence component of mental strength. This signifies your ability to identify and seize opportunities. If you are confident in yourself and your abilities and can engage easily with others, you are also more likely to convert challenging situations into successful outcomes (Ribeiro, 2019).

Exercise: The 5-Minute Technique

Remember that brilliant technique I mentioned my friend had shared with me? Well, here it is:

In order to use the five-minute, three-column technique, you need to know the ten most common forms of self-talk or cognitive distortions. I'll remind you of what those are here so that you don't have to page back.

1. Black and white thinking
2. Overgeneralization
3. Filtering
4. Disqualifying the positives
5. Jumping to conclusions
6. Minimizing or magnifying
7. Emotional reasoning
8. "Should" statements
9. Labeling and mislabeling
10. Personalizing

This technique can be done mentally, but it works far better when you put it down in writing. The technique works well at any time of the day or when you are particularly conflicted, but it's most effective first thing in the morning to get yourself into the right mindset or last thing at night so that you can rest easy with a clear mind.

Step 1: Draw three columns on a piece of paper (use whatever medium that would work best for you, e.g., tech heads can do this in Excel if they want to).

Step 2: In the first column, record the piece of negative self-talk that is concerning you. Keep it simple, and be sure to record the first thing that springs to mind, as that is usually the most pressing issue to be dealt with. Examples of such thoughts could be, "I had an awful day," "My health is deteriorating, I'm sure there is something very wrong with me," or, "My boss thinks I'm useless."

Step 3: Next up, read the statement you've just written down. It often makes a huge difference to see your negative thoughts in writing. Try to ascertain which cognitive distortions your thought fits and write that down in the second column. It is very likely that your thoughts will not fit neatly into just one distortion. Feel free to list as many as you need to in order to describe the nature of your negative self-talk clearly.

Step 4: Lastly, you will record your logical response to this negative self-talk and your acknowledgment of the cognitive distortion it represents in the third column. As an example, a rational response to "I had an awful day" could be, "Actually, only one challenging thing happened to me this morning, but I allowed that event to color the rest of my day. Many positive things happened, but I didn't focus on those things."

You can use this exercise for as many thoughts as you like at one time. The secondary benefit of this is that you will start to catch yourself in the thought pattern as it happens, and you will be able to use your discoveries from this exercise to reduce the effect that negative thinking has on you in real-time.

Here's an example:

Column 1: The piece of negative self-talk you identify is, "I am not good at my job." This piece of self-talk has been coming up a lot lately since you were promoted to a new position. It's taken you some time to adjust to your new tasks, and you feel like you've made too many mistakes. Every time a task comes up that you struggle with, you notice that this thought comes up, impacting your self-confidence and ability to do your job.

Column 2: You consider this thought and, based on the evidence at hand, decide that it is a case of filtering. Instead of focusing on the fact that you were promoted because you are very qualified to do the job and that there is always going to be a learning curve to adjust to a new position, you're focusing only on the fact that you have made a few mistakes. You have also received good feedback from your boss about your progress so far. Despite this, you have filtered out all of the good stuff, and you're focusing only on the bad stuff.

Column 3: Having acknowledged that this thought falls under a cognitive distortion, you can now analyze it based on what you logically know about the situation. You know that your boss believed in you enough to promote you in the first place. You also understand that it is very natural to experience a learning curve in a new role and that there is no way that you will execute every task perfectly the first time. Finally, if you allow yourself to look at everything you've done so far without filtering, you must acknowledge that you are doing quite well. So your reframed thought for this piece of negative self-talk could be, "I am new to this role, and just like anyone else, I need to learn all the new tasks. I have the skills to do this, and I am doing well so far. I will make mistakes, but that is part of learning. Next time I will be completing the task with greater knowledge."

Identified Negative Self-Talk

Cognitive Distortion Identified

Corrected Self-Talk

"I am not good at my job."

Filtering

"I am new to this role, and just like anyone else, I need to learn all the new tasks. I have the skills to do this, and I am doing well so far. I will make mistakes, but that is part of learning. Next time I will be completing the task with greater knowledge."

> *"If there is no struggle, there is no progress."*
>
> — FREDERICK DOUGLASS

5

YOU ARE WHO YOU THINK YOU ARE —COGNITIVE DEFUSION

I had mentioned before that Cognitive Behavioral Therapy became a major part of my journey away from toxic thinking. As is always the case, certain components of this therapy and Acceptance and Commitment Therapy (ACT) were more impactful than others. As every person attending therapy is different, and they are trying to resolve such varied challenges, there is never a one-size-fits-all treatment plan. The components of CBT and ACT that I share in this book are tools that I have found particularly helpful in challenging negative self-talk.

One such concept is cognitive defusion, which I will discuss in more detail in this chapter.

You Are Who You Think You Are

The idea that we build up about ourselves in our heads is extremely powerful. When we practice habitual, repetitive negative thinking and this thought process becomes automatic, the perception we create in our minds of ourselves becomes fused with our identity. Even though these thoughts are just creating an alternate perception of reality, through this fusing process, the self-image we have created becomes the reality that we project out onto the world.

A study conducted in 2013 illustrates how the idea we have of ourselves significantly influences the way we interact with the world (Mead, 2019). Researchers needed to focus the study on a group of people they knew to have a self-image that did not match their reality. People living with eating disorders are, for the most part, known to have an image of themselves created in their minds that does not match up with reality. It is for this reason that researchers used a group of people living with anorexia for this study. A control group of people that had never reported any diagnosis of eating disorders was used as well. The task given to the groups was a rather mundane one—they were asked to navigate their way through doorways of different widths. That's all they had to do. Of course, it was not the task that was being observed, it was each group's behavior during the task that was the key to the researcher's findings. The study showed that the control group started to turn their shoulders at the door frame that was 25% wider than their shoulders. On the other hand, the group of people living with eating disorders already started to turn their shoulders at the doorway that was 40% wider than their shoulders. This showed that those with anorexia had created a picture in their minds of their bodies being larger than they were in reality, which impacted the way they interacted with the world around them. These people believed that their bodies were physically larger than they are because of the language they habitually used to describe themselves in their self-talk.

Another study conducted in 2004 by researchers Conroy and Metzler demonstrated the impact of self-talk in athletes (Mead, 2019). The researchers, in this case, focused on the self-talk experienced by athletes in situations in which they were failing, succeeding, hoping to succeed, or fearing failure. The type of self-talk they experienced in each situation was recorded. Additionally, researchers measured various situation-specific types of performance anxiety, such as fear of success, fear of failure, and sports anxiety. Results showed that anxiety levels were far higher when the athletes experienced negative self-talk around sports anxiety and fear of failure.

So, regardless of the emotional state the athlete found themselves in—failure, success, hoping to succeed, or fearing failure—their anxiety levels were consistently higher if they had also been experiencing negative self-talk. An athlete that won a race, for example, but was also practicing negative self-talk, would experience higher levels of anxiety than an athlete that had lost the race if the losing athlete was practicing positive self-talk.

In my journey to dig my way out of my toxic thinking hole, I had to practice distancing myself from the toxic thinking that was constantly bubbling up in my mind. I would come to learn that this distancing would be achieved through cognitive defusion. Now, if you are picturing a bomb disposal unit carefully approaching and defusing a ticking time bomb in your head, you're not far off.

Really though, cognitive defusion is just a fancy term for distancing oneself from negative thinking. Just as we have discussed using meditation and mindfulness to become observers of our thoughts, cognitive defusion is about putting distance between yourself and the constant chatter that is happening in your head. In other words, "This conversation is interesting to observe and may hold some value, but it is not a reflection of who I am." By doing this, we reduce the impact that our self-talk has on our lives.

Cognitive defusion can be beneficial in some of the following circumstances:

- Getting rid of deeply ingrained cognitive biases, distortions, and negative perceptions.
- Overcoming addictions or compulsive urges.
- When attempting to overcome cognitive distortions that cause you to misrepresent the scale of a problem

or allow you to become blind to the reality of a situation.

- Overcoming repetitive and persistent thoughts that have become automatic. An example of this is the phrase "Mary had a little ____" —it is very likely that you did not have to even finish reading the sentence to be able to complete it with the word "lamb." You know this because you have heard it so many times. We can leverage this same type of automatic thinking in reverse and train ourselves to think the automatic thoughts of our choosing.
- When FEAR has become an obstacle to your success. The acronym FEAR stands for **F**using with your thoughts; **E**valuating the experience; **A**voiding the experience; **R**eason provisioning for your behavior.

When we are dealing with long-standing cognitive distortions, using restructuring (thinking differently about the bias) does not work. It can be described best by saying that you can't expect to see a different view if both you and your distortion are looking out of the same window. Therefore it's important for us to differentiate between negative self-talk, which impacts our daily lives but has not yet become fused into our sense of identity, as the type of long-standing distortion we refer to here. In dealing with longstanding cognitive distortions, cognitive defusion is key.

When we deal with distortions of a scaling variety, such as catastrophizing, or those of a blinding variety, such as filtering, cognitive defusion is also helpful. By distancing ourselves from the idea that the worst-case scenario will always happen and simply observing the situation for what it is, we can more clearly see that the catastrophe is not necessarily the reality.

Equally, with blinding distortions, when we can simply observe the situation rather than feel that we are directed by it, it is easier to view both the positive and negative aspects of a situation.

Repetitive thoughts often become automatic and, as a result, cause us to behave in a way that is controlled by the distortion and not by our logical thinking or choice. Cognitive defusion can help you to look at examples of prior experiences in order to assess the situation realistically.

The FEAR acronym is commonly used in both ACT and CBT, and when we break down the components of the acronym, it is easy to see why cognitive defusion would be so helpful here.

We know the F in FEAR stands for "fusing with your thoughts," and this one makes the use of cognitive defusion a no-brainer. The antidote to fusion must be defusion, after all.

The E in FEAR represents how you evaluate the experience at hand. This comes down to the perception you create in your mind of an event, depending on the label you assign to it. Through cognitive defusion, you can observe a situation from a distance rather than feeling as though you need to experience it at an emotional level.

The A in FEAR stands for your avoidance of the situation. This happens when you go out of your way to avoid an event—whether in the past or future—because you don't want to face it. This not only prevents you from dealing with past trauma, but it also stunts your growth, as you may miss out on future opportunities. By using the cognitive defusion technique, you will be able to view these past and future opportunities from the perspective of an observer and thereby gain greater objectivity over them.

Finally, the R in FEAR stands for the reasons you provide for your behavior. As human beings, we love to explain things and provide reasons for them, even when we don't need to. If you turn down a friend's invitation to go to an event that does not interest you, that is completely acceptable. You do not need to spend the next few days justifying that decision in your head—yet so often, we do. By using cognitive defusion, you will be able to view your decision not to attend the event from the perspective of an unbiased party and, hopefully, recognize that your decision was fair and does not require any justification neither for your friend nor the voice in your head.

Parting Ways: Cognitive Defusion Techniques

Cognitive defusion is a combination of thinking strategies and mental activities that help to reduce the impact of unwanted and negative thoughts. The purpose of cognitive defusion is to help you see that your thoughts are just strings of words and not judgments or facts. The techniques used in cognitive defusion help you distance yourself from toxic thinking by altering the function of the stimulus. In this context, the stimulus is the negative thought itself, and the function refers to the impact it has on us, whether that is the experience of emotional pain, the impact on your self-image, or how deeply you believe your thoughts.

Through cognitive defusion, you can change the context in which thoughts occur rather than trying to change the nature of the thought. In using cognitive defusion, you no longer become one with your thoughts, but, instead, you can be an outside-looking-in observer of those thoughts. By distancing yourself in this manner, you can reduce the impact that negative thoughts have on your life. For the most part, you learn to accept the thoughts for what they are—ideas, words, and pictures—rather than assigning them a value and allowing your biases and inner critic to create judgment around them. Cognitive defusion does not make negative thoughts go away; instead, it reduces their credibility so that you can continue to have them but not be impacted by them.

Cognitive Defusion Techniques

Cognitive defusion is a concept in ACT and CBT, and it can be achieved through several different techniques. The technique/s you choose will depend on your particular situation, your personality, and the nature of your negative thoughts. The following are a few evidence-based cognitive defusion techniques.

Titchener's Emotional Word Repetition Strategy

This technique is one of the first that was developed around cognitive defusion and has been shown to have the greatest results. The main idea behind this repetition strategy is to repeat a word or sentence which represents your negative thought out loud, over and over, until it has lost its meaning and power over you. Let's face it—words are powerful, we know this, but really, it is the meaning we place upon those words that have the real power and not the word itself. It is the negativity the word triggers that impacts you, not the collection of letters.

I am sure that you've experienced the phenomenon of a word not seeming like a word anymore when you've said it enough times. Before you get to the actual words that are bothering you, you can start with something mundane like "tree" or "face." Say the word continuously for 45 seconds and see how you begin to feel about it. It sounds strange, doesn't it? Almost like it has no meaning anymore. It's suddenly just a series of sounds that you are making that doesn't necessarily refer to something with bark and leaves or eyes and a nose. That is the point you want to get to with your negative words and thoughts. When you can start to experience those seemingly powerful words as nothing more than a series of sounds, you will start to reduce the impact the word has on you. Research has shown that by using Titchener's Repetition Method, you can reduce the discomfort within 10 seconds of repetition and reduce the believability of the word within 30 seconds (The Authentic Model, n.d.).

Before engaging in this technique, it's important to remember that it is not the word itself that has a negative impact on you; it is the meaning you assign to it. Let's use the word "fat" as an example. In essence, the word describes nothing more than a specific type of tissue in a mammal's body, but it has an entire world of connotations behind it. These connotations, and the meaning we assign to them, have a negative impact on us, especially when we use them as a label for ourselves. In some people's minds, "fat" also means *unhealthy, failure, lazy, loser,* and even *ugly*. For people struggling with weight issues, the word "fat" can become an anchor for a considerable amount of self-reproach, but it's just a word. Ridiculously, when we use the word in a sentence to imply overweight, it doesn't even make sense—"You are fat." No, I am a human being made up of muscle, bone, tissue, and, yes, some fat.

By using the repetition method of cognitive defusion, you can start to see the word "fat" (or whichever word or phrase you choose) for what it is—just a word. Want to know how this works? Well, one theory is that every time you repeat the word, a neuron in your brain fires, and, over time, the stimuli lose their potency. This effect is called reactive inhibition (Shukla, 2019).

Turn "I Am..." Into "I Notice..."

This cognitive defusion technique is particularly effective for recurring thoughts that cause you emotional pain. By using this technique, you harness the power of distancing language to turn experiences into observations. When you use language that denotes that you are experiencing a thought as reality ("I am so stupid"), you turn that thought into your reality. As a result, you feel emotions that are linked to that reality, such as shame and reduced self-confidence. When you use distancing language ("I notice I am feeling that what I did was stupid"), you no longer have to experience that as your reality. Instead, you are simply observing this thought as though it were happening to someone else, and it is easier for you to have a more realistic perspective of the negative self-talk.

Change Context and Perspective by Using Metaphors

Quick English refresher before we get into this technique's explanation:

> *"A metaphor is a figure of speech that describes an object or action in a way that isn't literally true, but helps explain an idea or make a comparison." -* (Underwood, 2018)

In this cognitive defusion technique, we use metaphors to give context to our thoughts. The metaphor that you assign to something (a thought, emotion, or event) plays a large role in how you experience it. Take happiness, for instance. There are many metaphors to assign to happiness: some call it a journey, and others call it a destination. Still, others might refer to it as a creation. Depending on which of these conceptualizations you pick, your experience of happiness will likely differ. If you use the journey metaphor, you may stumble upon happiness along the path of your life. If you use the destination metaphor, you will be focused on finding happiness. Finally, if you use the creation metaphor, you will believe that you can make your own happiness.

This metaphorical conceptualization works for both positive and negative thoughts, and when we use metaphors in cognitive defusion, we can consciously choose a comparison that suits our needs. Positive beliefs could be like a house made of bricks and mortar—very difficult to destroy. Negative beliefs could be like a house made of paper—extremely easy to blow over, and it can be burned to ashes with a single spark.

For the most part, when you pick a metaphor for a negative thought, you want it to be something that you are familiar with and that personally works for what you are trying to achieve.

Rate Your Thoughts

In this cognitive defusion technique, we start with a thought that we know is believable and does not cause us emotional pain (remember that stimulus function idea we discussed earlier in this section?). This controlled thought can be as simple as: "I am a human being." That is highly realistic, and unless you're having an anti-human day, it should cause you very little emotional pain; so, if you were to rate this thought on a scale of 1 to 100, where would it go? Probably at 100, right? It's 100% believable.

Now use this same scale for other thoughts that you observe in your mind. Use your critical thinking skills to gain a good perspective of your thoughts before you rate them. Consider the thought, "I am dumb." That's a nasty one, but it pops into most people's minds regularly, especially if you are particularly hard on yourself and you've made a mistake. Consider this thought from the perspective of your life. Perhaps you've had your IQ tested at some stage, that's pretty good evidence of reality. You have a job, manage to conduct relationships, and, guess what...you're reading this book, so there is clearly nothing wrong with your level of intelligence. This particularly unbelievable thought that will cause you significant emotional pain should be a zero rating; but, since our scale starts at 1, we'll go with that.

Now you have a good idea of what a believable thought looks like on the rating scale, as well as what an unbelievable and unhelpful thought looks like. You can now go ahead and use this technique to rate all of your thoughts and gain a new perspective on them.

Use a Third Person Perspective to Voice Your Thoughts

An excellent way to regulate the emotions you experience from negative thoughts is by rephrasing them in the third person. The cognitive defusion technique helps to create distance between you and the thought by making you the owner of the thought rather than the person experiencing it. People that own things can choose what they do with them. When you own your thoughts in the third person, you can choose whether you want to interact with them or simply observe them.

As an example, we can think of a thought about our day in the first person, "I had a terrible day," and experience that thought and its accompanying pain first hand; or you can rephrase it in the third person, "She had a terrible day," or "Sally had a terrible day," but, of course, use your own name!

This cognitive defusion technique does not change the meaning of the thought, but it creates distance between you and it.

Stop, Step Back, and Observe

This cognitive defusion technique includes many aspects of mindfulness and meditation. It is beneficial if you find yourself brooding, repeating, or becoming obsessed with unhelpful thoughts. By using this technique, you can help to shift your mood and ease rumination. The first step is to instruct yourself—out loud if you need to—to stop. This means stopping both your mental and physical activities. If you are sitting down, stand up, and vice versa. Next up, you want to step back. To do this, you need to change your context. You can leave the room that you are in at the time or simply visualize yourself being somewhere else. While you want to walk away from your unhelpful thoughts, you don't want to ignore them.

Lastly, remind yourself that you are not your thought, you are simply experiencing the thought. The thought does not define you. Take the time to observe all of the sensations that are connected with the situation. Using all your senses, get a deep understanding of the context of your thought in this particular situation and then start the process of mindfully accepting it from the perspective of an observer. Remind yourself that your experience is happening in the present moment. You can now begin to start the process of finding a new perspective, challenging assumptions, finding actual evidence to support your feelings, and refuting those that do not fit in reality.

Replace Your Inner Critic with a Funny Voice

There is no doubt that humor helps us cope with emotional difficulties, but research shows that it can also help us change the perspective of the contents of a thought into something that is easier to deal with. Think about your mean boss saying, "You are so stupid!" That hurts, right? It's painful to think about, and you're likely also feeling many other emotions around that thought. Now try to picture Goofy (Yes! The Disney character) saying it, or even Bart Simpson. Does it have as much of an impact on you? Does it have any impact at all, or are you just giggling? The content of the thought has not changed, all that has changed is the context of the thought.

Slow Down Your Thoughts

This cognitive defusion technique leverages the speed at which we sound out thoughts and how, by slowing them down, we change what they mean to us and even how those thoughts make us feel.

One of the main reasons that negative thoughts cause anxiety is the rapid fire at which they assail our brains. Before we know it, we've thought a huge number of anxiety-inducing thoughts that, although difficult to separate if you aren't practicing mindfulness, still have an impact on us.

The idea of this technique is to slow the wording of your thought down. So if it ordinarily takes you two seconds to sound out one word of the string in the thought, slow that down to six seconds, or even 10 seconds. Slow it down and drag it out. Then, notice how that same thought changes the meaning. In some cases, it may even completely lose its meaning. It is going to sound completely ridiculous, and that is the whole point! If we are honest, most of these negative thoughts we have are ridiculous anyway, so it seems fitting that they should sound that way and, in the process, lose their impact on us. By controlling the speed at which you think or say the thought, you also gain control over its effects on you.

Focus on the Power of Choice

One of the most powerful parts of the human experience is our choice. As much as we would like to believe that things outside of our reach control us, we always have a choice. We may not have a choice about the types of experiences that present themselves in our lives, but we do have a choice in how we react to those experiences.

The same applies to the experience of our thoughts. We can choose how we experience both our positive and our negative thoughts. The cognitive defusion technique that relates to this power of choice that we have is best achieved by replacing the word "but" with the word "and" and the word "can't" with the phrase "I am choosing not to."

An example of this could be, "I would like to stop smoking cigarettes, but I can't," which when we apply this technique becomes, "I would like to stop smoking cigarettes, and I choose not to." See how that puts the responsibility for the behavior as well as the power of choice right back into your court?

Label Your Thoughts

Just as you may use labels negatively in your self-talk, you can also use them against your negative self-talk to change their context and distance yourself from them. You can use various types of labels to categorize your thoughts and create distance. The first thing you can look at is the type of thought you are having. Is it a fantasy, memory, distortion, a blame statement, or a question? If you have specific thoughts that you regularly experience, you can create names for those thoughts. An example could be if you regularly have a negative thought about your appearance, you could call this the Good Looking Thought (the irony is intentional, of course, but not required).

When you get used to labeling your thoughts in this way, you can also combine this technique with others. For example, consider phrasing the labels you give your thoughts in a manner that distances them from you even more, such as "I notice that my mind is presenting the Good Looking Thought," or, "I notice that my mind is creating a blame statement."

This technique helps you understand that the thoughts your mind creates are, for the most part, not helpful to you. However, what is useful is using your logical mind to counter the negative impact these thoughts might have by learning to label them accurately.

There are several benefits to using defusion techniques to disconnect ourselves from our thoughts. These include:

- Thoughts with a negative connotation become less believable and less impactful on our emotional state.
- We can control our thoughts.

- Words lose their negative connotation and become simply a series of sounds.
- We can zoom out and observe our thoughts from an alternative perspective.
- We can reduce our emotional attachment to some of our beliefs, which helps to facilitate a more pragmatic view of our thoughts and our lives in general.
- It becomes easier to challenge existing negative ideas in our minds.

The cognitive defusion process, and the techniques we've discussed here, are extremely useful in eliminating toxic thinking in our lives; but it is just another part of the process that I would come to learn is the key to digging yourself out of the toxic thinking hole forever.

The follow-up to cognitive defusion is the cognitive restructuring process.

"Forget the mistake. Remember the lesson."

— UNKNOWN

6

THE METAMORPHOSIS OF TOXIC THINKING—COGNITIVE RESTRUCTURING

Now that we understand the cognitive defusion process and we know how to start distancing ourselves from these negative thoughts, we can move on to the next part of the process that I've found to be so helpful in digging my way out of toxic thinking. The next phase is cognitive restructuring which is also known as cognitive reframing. This is a core structure within the concepts of Cognitive Behavioral Therapy (CBT).

In this chapter, we will discuss the practice of cognitive restructuring. We will find out why it is such an important follow-up to cognitive defusion, why it is so beneficial, and the techniques that are used in cognitive restructuring.

What Is Cognitive Restructuring?

Cognitive restructuring is a part of the therapeutic process which involves replacing or modifying negative thoughts as well as some of the automatic beliefs that we have about ourselves.

When I was on this journey, during the cognitive defusion process, I found myself identifying and distancing myself from the chaos that often raged within me due to negative and toxic thinking. After working on defusion for some time, my therapist suggested that I move on to the process of restructuring my thoughts so that I could cultivate positive and healthier thought habits. So, essentially, I had managed to start distancing myself from these thoughts, but that only helped for so long, and at some point, I had to fill the void that I had created in that distancing process with something better. I was choosing to replace the bad with the good.

I will admit that when my therapist told me that I was ready to move to phase two of my journey, I was a little confused. I had just done all of this work to break down the fusion between my identity and my thoughts. I had spent a considerable amount of time learning cognitive defusion techniques, and I felt I had made significant progress. My therapist helped me to see, though, that there were still some niggly negative thoughts, the ones that I had been holding onto for a lot of my life that needed more work and a different approach.

Through cognitive defusion, I had been able to distance myself from much of the negative thinking that had been taxing my energy and holding me back, but there were a few thoughts that had their roots so deep in my psyche that defusion had not been enough. My therapist gave me an analogy to explain how the two therapeutic processes worked together to solve the toxic thinking conundrum. She describes the negative thoughts in my mind as parasites in a system.

Some of the parasites had deep roots, and others had shallow roots. When I had started practicing cognitive defusion, I had essentially flushed the system and learned how to neutralize those parasites. This worked really well on most of the parasites (the ones with shallow roots), but the ones with deeper roots that had been growing for longer were simply stunned for a little while by this neutralizing process. By using cognitive restructuring, I could send out a flood of kryptonite to the stronger parasites, hitting them until they were neutralized. Eventually, their roots lost hold on the system, and they withered away and replaced it with organisms that were beneficial to the system.

Through this analogy, I understood that both of these processes were vital to the long-term demolition of toxic thinking. One method paved the way, and the other cements the change.

I know very well that attempting to change your thoughts can sometimes seem like an intimidating and possibly impossible task. I know this because I have experienced that intimidation first hand and overcame it. I managed to overcome it by framing the process as building a new skill. My old thought processes had been a learned skill even though I hadn't known that I was learning it at the time. So in setting out to restructure the way I thought, I approached it like I was taking a course to develop myself. If you are learning a skill like playing guitar or cooking, you simply follow the steps and practice as much as possible until you have learned the skill, and this is exactly how I suggest you approach this process.

The process only becomes intimidating or impossible when you make it that way. So don't focus on the fancy psychological terms. They are good to know, but it's the directions and instructions that will help you to achieve your goals.

Transforming The Knots: Cognitive Restructuring Techniques

There are four steps that need to be followed to restructure negative thoughts into positive ones. I want to point out that positive thoughts don't necessarily have to equate to happy thoughts. We are being realistic here, and I'm not trying to turn your head into an episode of The Brady Bunch. When I refer to positive thoughts, I mean thoughts that are not toxic to you. Positive thoughts are helpful, less critical, and help to boost self-confidence rather than break it down.

Step One: Identify Thoughts That Have Become Automatic

While not all automatic thoughts are negative, and some can be helpful or driven by instinct, some do fall into the highly unhelpful and toxic realm. Negative Automatic Thoughts

(NATs) are a concept we've discussed before in this book. They are toxic and often difficult to identify. NATs often take the form of vague, negative statements such as, "I am stupid," "Everyone hates me," or "I always screw up." These thoughts often occur, lack any real precision, and often describe events that have not yet happened. They also always cause emotional distress, even though it may not be entirely noticeable at the time.

Mindfulness and meditation are both excellent ways to help identify NATs as both methods allow us to cut out the white noise and determine which of our thoughts need to be focused on. This is not going to be an easy thing to do. Halting yourself in the middle of an emotional experience to analyze your thoughts takes practice and focus, but it is entirely possible to achieve.

You can start this by consciously turning on your internal alarm system for negative emotions. Remind yourself to increase your awareness any time you feel something that could be considered negative. Then work your way backward and identify what thoughts are accompanying those emotions. Where did it all start? You may start to find that many of these negative emotional experiences are triggered by similar thoughts. These thoughts are often not conscious and seep into your mind without your knowledge. Something else you may find very interesting is how the same NAT triggers many different negative emotional experiences. Once you can identify and work on that NAT, you'll be able to eliminate many different negative reactions.

Another good way to identify your NATs is through self-compassion, acceptance, and the reduction of self-judgment. We all often react in ways that are OTT and simply not fitting, but there is no need to chastise yourself for that. Instead, accept that it is a very human reaction and one that you can work on and change now that you've acknowledged it.

Step Two: Address Cognitive Distortions

Some NATs will fall into the cognitive distortion category. These are usually flawed, misrepresented, or disrupted thoughts. Many cognitive distortions are classified as biases where you tend to think a certain way, leading to inaccurate conclusions. We discussed a variety of cognitive distortions and biases in chapter 2. By learning to identify these in your own thinking, you can start to zoom out from your own head and catch yourself in the act of developing these unhelpful thought patterns.

Step Three: Socratic Questioning

This technique is named after Socrates, the Greek philosopher credited with being one of the founders of Western philosophical tenets. Socrates developed a teaching technique that involved him asking his students questions so that they could arrive at the answers themselves. He believed that the disciplined practice of thoughtful questions allowed his students the opportunity to discover the validity of their ideas (Wikipedia Contributors, 2019a).

In our context, we use this technique to ask ourselves questions to counter NATs and cognitive distortions. When you identify either as a NAT or a cognitive distortion in your thinking, ask yourself a question about it.

Some of these questions may include:

1. Why would you say that?
2. How does this relate to your experience?
3. What assumptions am I making here?
4. Are there any other ways for me to interpret this?
5. How does this make me feel?
6. What do I believe that this means?
7. Is this thought based on reality?
8. Is this thought based on feelings or facts?
9. What evidence supports this thought?
10. Is there a possibility that I am misinterpreting this?

Socratic questioning can help you to gain a new perspective and interpret negative thoughts in new ways so that they can be transformed into something useful.

Identify a thought that you feel needs to be questioned. There is always at least one thought that you think could be irrational or destructive, and very often, it pops into your head quite regularly. Once you have isolated this thought, consider what evidence there is for and against the validity of the thought. With the evidence at hand, you are able to make a logical decision about the thought and determine whether facts or feelings cause it. Next, ask yourself if this thought is a black and white situation. Are there perhaps shades of grey in between that need to be taken into account. Are you perhaps making something straightforward into something that is overly complex? Could you be misinterpreting the evidence that you are looking at, or is it plain to see? Now, think about how others might see this situation. Would another individual's interpretation be similar to or different from yours, and how so? Are you choosing to only look at some evidence and turning a blind eye to other evidence?

Step Four: Accept Rational Conclusions

As a follow-up to Socratic questioning, the interpretations you have taken from the process now need to be assessed based on how rational they are. You will use either anecdotal evidence or objective evidence to support a new and more positive interpretation of your thought. It is not necessary to accept these new interpretations simply because they have presented themselves during the process, and it is important to have evidence to support your belief. After all, it was blindly believing your toxic thinking patterns without questioning their validity for all this time that has led you to this point. So, no more blind acceptance, from now on, we use critical thinking to assess our thoughts.

Once you can start making this process a habit, you find yourself able to question negative thoughts and distortions on the fly. You will also be able to keep a mental log of which thoughts are valid and can be stored and which are not. With enough practice, this will become second nature.

Bonus Exercise: Stay Calm and Reduce Stress and Anxiety

This exercise can be used in many different anxiety-inducing situations. It is particularly effective in social anxiety situations where you may be struggling to speak or interact with your colleagues at work, around a prospective partner, or in social situations like dinner parties. It helps to improve performance by reducing the impact that negative thoughts have on anxiety levels. The technique is often referred to as semantic conversion or thought conversion.

In any situation in which you feel anxiety or stress developing, you can apply the following two steps to ease those feelings and free yourself up to take part and perform to the best of your ability.

Step One: Mindful Labelling

Allow yourself to simply notice your thoughts and emotions. So often, we are aware of only a very small number of the thoughts that run through our minds and the emotions we experience. By forcing ourselves to become aware of these emotions, we can access a deeper thought layer. Once you have placed your awareness on these thoughts and emotions, start to label them in some of the ways we've previously discussed. Use the best descriptors that you can think of to label your thoughts. You may also find it helpful to ask yourself the following questions:

- What is making me anxious about this situation?
- What are the names of the emotions I am experiencing?
- Are the thoughts related to a specific person?
- Do I actually know what people are thinking?
- Do I have a realistic basis for forming these judgments?

By asking yourself these questions, you will be able to put your thoughts and emotions into words. Do your best to use constructive and positive words to label your thoughts. The mindful part of this activity simply relates to looking inward and being aware of your thoughts and emotions, not just how they physically make you feel.

Step Two: Constructive Rephrasing

The next step is to rephrase your thoughts in a way that helps to reduce your anxiety and stress. Rather than catastrophizing or limiting yourself through your thinking, use the evidence you have gathered around the reality of the thought to come up with a more helpful alternative. In this step, you want to use descriptors that provide clarity.

Here's an example:

You are getting ready to go on stage and present your research at a conference. This is your first time, and although your boss has said she has faith in you, you're experiencing a lot of stress and anxiety. The thought that you identify going through your head might sound something like this, "I am so nervous! I am sure this is going to completely tank. All those people are going to be staring at me, and I'm going to freeze."

In fairness, you have no idea whether you're going to do poorly at this presentation, and the evidence of your preparation and knowledge on the subject indicates that you will do well. There is no evidence that you will do badly or make any mistakes; that's just a negative, unfounded thought. All those people will be looking at you because they have chosen to attend your presentation as they think you have something valuable to say. So with those reasonings in mind, your restructured thought may sound something like this, "I do feel nervous, but this feeling can help me to focus. I've prepared well, and I know the subject matter inside out, so there is no reason for me not to be able to give these people the information they came for. All I have to do is focus on my research and nothing else."

When attempting to rephrase emotions, it can be helpful to rank the intensity of the emotion you are experiencing and choose a label from an emotional intensity set that is one or two levels down (whichever you are comfortable with) (Shukla, 2018).

Fear Emotions

Most Intense: Horrified, paralyzed, phobic, petrified, terrorized, dreaded, panicked, shocked.

Less Intense: Anxious, distrustful, alarmed, aversive, jumpy, fearful, perturbed, nervous, shaky, rattled, suspicious, unsettled, worried, wary, unnerved.

Least Intense: Alert, afraid, cautious, apprehensive, disconcerted, disquieted, edgy, doubtful, fidgety, hesitant, insecure, scared, leery, timid, watchful, uneasy.

Anger Emotions

Most intense: Appalled, aggressive, bitter, belligerent, disgusted, contemptuous, furious, hostile, hateful, livid, irate, menacing, outraged, raving, seething, spiteful, vengeful, vicious, violent, vindictive.

Less intense: Aggravated, affronted, antagonized, angry, exasperated, bristling, incensed, inflamed, indignant, mad, resentful, riled-up, offended.

Least intense: Apathetic, annoyed, crabby, cold, critical, cranky, detached, frustrated, displeased, peeved, indifferent.

Sadness Emotions

Most intense: Bereaved, anguished, depressed, bleak, despondent, hopeless, morose, despairing, heartbroken.

Less intense: Discouraged, dejected, down, dispirited, heavy-hearted, sorrowful, grieving, weepy, mournful, gloomy, melancholy.

Least intense: Disappointed, contemplative, regretful, listless, low, steady, distracted, wistful, disconnected.

Shame Emotions

Most intense: Degraded, belittled, demeaned, humiliated, ostracized, mortified, self-condemning.

Less intense: Chagrified, ashamed, culpable, contrite, guilty, embarrassed, humbled, penitent, intimidated, remorseful, rueful, reproachful, sheepish, rueful.

Least intense: Awkward, abashed, flustered, hesitant, reticent, withdrawn, speechless.

If you find that words are not sufficient to describe or rephrase your thought or emotion, feel free to use a series of words or even a sentence.

"Consistency is more important than perfection."

— MICHAEL HYATT

7

BLOWING OFF ESTEEM—MAKING WAY FOR POSITIVITY AND CONFIDENCE

As you start to reduce the hold that toxic thinking has on your life, you will be ready to start rebuilding your confidence and positivity levels. I know how low these aspects of ourselves are left in the wake of that wave of negative thinking. The hints and tips I will share in this chapter are some of the ways I helped improve my confidence and positivity when I got my toxic thinking under control.

The Psychological Importance of Positive Self-Talk

We already have a good understanding of what negative self-talk is, so that does help us to understand its opposite—positive self-talk. Positive self-talk does not mean that you are not realistic. In fact, by its very nature, positive self-talk is usually more fact-based and realistic than its counterpart. We have seen how negative self-talk feeds off our distortions and biases, all of which are rooted in false information. When we practice positive self-talk, we focus on encouraging helpful and hopeful thoughts that affirm that we can survive and thrive no matter what we are going through.

Positive self-talk is important because it can help us to improve our performance and our general well-being. It's not just good only for our mental health, though. As positive inner dialogue helps to reduce stress, it also allows us to avoid stress-related physical ailments. Some of the physical benefits you will see from practicing positive self-talk include:

- Increased levels of vitality
- Greater satisfaction levels
- Immune system boosts
- Reduction in pain levels
- Improved cardiovascular health
- Greater all-round physical well-being
- Increased longevity
- Lower levels of stress and anxiety

Perhaps the best way for us to understand what positive self-talk is is to pit it up against its counterpart. Here are some examples:

Negative form: "If I change my mind, everyone will be disappointed."

Positive form: "Those that care for me will understand if I change my mind. The choice is mine."

Negative form: "My failure is embarrassing."
Positive form: "I was brave enough to try, and I should be proud of myself for that, regardless of the outcome."

Negative form: "I am so fat and unfit, I may as well just stay here on the couch."
Positive form: "Regardless of my current physical state, I know that I am a strong and capable person. I deserve to be healthier."

Negative form: "I'm the reason we lost that game, and I've let the entire team down."
Positive form: "I play a team sport. Everyone in the team contributed, and everyone had the power to make a difference."

Negative form: "I have no idea how to do this new activity. I am going to completely tank."
Positive form: "This is an opportunity to learn a new skill. No matter what the outcome, I am going to learn and grow as a person."

Negative form: "This is never going to work."
Positive form: "There is an equal chance of succeeding as there is of failing. If I give it my best effort, I can make it work."

The power of positive self-talk has been acknowledged and even studied on many occasions. In 2007, researchers Kendall and Treadwell (Mead, 2019) explored how self-talk impacts anxiety levels. They found that reducing negative self-talk in children with an anxiety disorder diagnosis significantly helped increase treatment efficacy.

In 1993, researcher Wrisberg (Mead, 2019) also investigated how self-talk could help people learn by breaking down large chunks of information into smaller chunks to aid recall.

In 2012, Chopra (Mead, 2019) discovered that by giving students strategies to help them turn their negative self-talk into a more positive narrative, many could successfully change their negative thought processes. The students found value from these changes in both their lives and their studies.

A major review of research and literature surrounding self-talk was conducted in 2011 by Oliver, Todd, and Harvey (Mead, 2019). They found that positive self-talk was highly effective in creating changes at a cognitive and behavioral level.

15 Ways to Make Positive Self-Talk a Habit

The following tips are all methods I've implemented in my own life to great effect. Some will work really well for you, and others may be less effective, but you will only know when you try.

Tip #1: Have a Purpose Bigger than Yourself

Research has shown that believing in something bigger than yourself can help to improve self-esteem and self-belief. This doesn't necessarily have to mean a religious belief in a specific higher power, either. If you find a cause that makes you feel like you are making a difference, this can have the same effect.

Feeling that you have a purpose helps you to focus on the positive things in life, and the more you focus on positivity, the more positive experiences you will have.

Research has found that purpose-driven people (Warrell, n.d.):

- Are four times more likely to be highly engaged at work
- 50% more likely to be a leader
- Have 64% higher level of career satisfaction
- Have a higher net worth and earn a higher income
- Enjoy 42% more contentment overall and live up to 7 years longer

As human beings, we are wired for far more than just survival. Once our basic human needs and desires are met, increasing wealth has a diminishing incremental impact on our happiness (that's right, more money can actually make you less happy). That's because once we go beyond basic needs, other more complex needs come into play, and money can't always meet those needs. When our highest purpose is focused only on accruing security and status, it may give a short-term boost to our ego, but it can also force us to continue living in the shallows. We may be unwilling to lay our pride on the line for the contribution, connection, and deep meaning we want the most.

While it would be nice to be able to find your purpose with a quick Google search, the reality is that our purpose tends to evolve and unfold as we do. Sometimes we have to sit in an open expanse of wondering in order to discover what has been staring us in the face the entire time. Experience has taught me that our purpose usually sits in the crossover between what we care about most and where we can contribute the most to helping others.

Tip #2: Remove Toxic People from Your Life

Sometimes it's difficult to know when someone is truly toxic in your life. I found that the best way to figure this out is when you feel relief when that person is not around. Unfortunately, these types of people come in many forms, and sometimes they are even family members. Highly negative and toxic people are energy vampires, though, and they will drag you back into a toxic thinking pit. No matter who these people are, it is vital to either completely remove them from your life or significantly limit the amount of time you spend with them.

How do you know when a person is toxic, though? A Los Angeles therapist who specializes in relationships, Barrie Sueskind, shares some of the key signs of toxicity (Raypole, 2019):

- self-centeredness or self-absorption
- manipulation and other types of emotional abuse
- deceit and dishonesty
- difficulty being compassionate to others
- a tendency to create conflict or drama

Some people tend to see themselves as the victim in every single situation. If they make a mistake, they might shift the blame to someone else or invent a story that paints them in a more positive light. This doesn't necessarily have to be a fabricated story, sometimes it's just their version of the truth with a few tweaks. In situations like this, you may feel tempted to nod and smile just to prevent an angry outburst. This may feel like your safest option, but it can also encourage a toxic person to see you as a supporter of their fabrications. Instead, try to disagree respectfully. You may want to say something like, "I had a different view on the situation," and describe what you feel happened. Just stick to the actual facts without pointing any fingers or making accusations. While your disagreement may make you unpopular with the toxic person or may upset them, it could also reduce the chances that they will try to involve you again.

Dealing with a person's toxic behavior can be downright exhausting. They might constantly complain about others, always have a new story about how they have been unfairly treated, or sometimes even accuse you of not caring about their needs or wronging them. In situations like this, resist the urge to jump on the complaining train with them or to immediately defend yourself against the accusations. Instead, respond with a simple, "I'm sorry you feel that way," and leave it at that.

Tip #3: Practice Gratitude

Gratitude journaling is a great way to remind yourself, each and every day, just how many things you have to be grateful for in your life. This can be a great blessing when you need to fight off negative thoughts, as it's difficult to be negative when there are so many positive things in your life. These don't always need to be big things. There are many small things to be grateful for, too, and these should be acknowledged. By expressing your gratitude in writing, you make these experiences tangible, and your brain will start to focus more on positivity.

Being excited about the benefits of gratitude can be a great thing because it gives us the kickstart we need to start making changes; however, we need to remain realistic about our goals.

Mental contrasting is the idea of being optimistic about the benefits of a new habit while also being realistic about how difficult building that habit may be. When we want to achieve something, using the technique of mental contrasting can lead us to exert more effort than is necessary or appropriate. In developing this habit, we need to recognize and plan for some of the obstacles that may get in our way. For example, if we know we tend to be exhausted at night, accept that it might not be the best time to focus and, instead, schedule our gratitude session for the morning time.

Tip #4: Stop Comparing Yourself to Everyone Else

This was a huge one for me. I lost a lot of self-esteem by comparing myself to other people, especially with social media making it so easy to get a view into other people's lives. I think a big wake-up call for me was my class reunion. I had quite a few ex-schoolmates on my social media, and I felt like they were way ahead of me in life. Their profiles showed simply perfect existences—exciting jobs, vacations in amazing destinations, loving partners, perfect children. Honestly, it's a miracle that I ended up going to my reunion because, at that point, my self-esteem was at an all-time low, and I was sure that I was going to feel even worse afterward. Boy, was I wrong. I won't say that I walked out of my reunion feeling like a million dollars, but I learned a pretty important lesson. Every single person that I had been comparing myself to online and against whom I had come to believe I was so lacking had their own challenges they were living with. Some were open about their challenges in our conversations throughout the night, others simply exuded sadness in person, despite the flashy life of perfection they portrayed in their posts and stories.

I also realized that it is pointless to compare yourself to anyone else because, even if you start at the same point, everyone is dealing with a different journey. Some will have challenges early in life, others later on. But, in the end, as the song says, the race is only with ourselves.

Tip #5: Use Positive Language when Speaking with Others

If we use negative language when speaking to others, we are more likely to use those same words in our self-talk. Start to make a conscious choice to speak positivity into the lives of others so that your own internal dialogue can start to match that. Think about the conversations you regularly have with others. Do you try to bond over negativity? Do you find it easier to have conversations with other people if you are both sharing some miserable experience? How can you change this? When you walk into your workplace on a Monday morning, what is the first conversation that you have about? Do you relay what you did on the weekend and how sad you are that the weekend is over and you have to come to work again? If so, you've taken the positivity of enjoying your weekend and not only tarnished it with the negativity of it being over, but you've also set the tone for the rest of the day, week, and perhaps even the month by verbalizing your negative ideas about it. You have not only spoken that negativity into the other person's life but also into your own. While it is completely normal to lament the ending of the weekend, it is not necessary to also complain about having to be at work. Instead, you could choose (yes, you have a choice) to celebrate the fact that you have a job to pay the bills and that it's a beautiful day.

Also linked to this is how we treat the ones we love. Has it become easier for you to focus on the negative aspects of your relationships with your loved ones? Do you mostly spew negativity at your spouse or your children? How then do you think that you will be able to focus on positivity yourself? Rather than focusing on the negative parts of your loved ones, choose to focus on their positive aspects and watch them grow. The other benefit of choosing to focus on the positivity in others is that they will be more likely to do so in return. When they see you choosing to be positive, they will be encouraged to make this choice too.

Tip #6: Believe in Your Own Success

So often, our biggest stumbling block to our own success is our self-doubt. If you don't believe in yourself, there is little chance that you will succeed. It is vital to believe in the capability that you have to succeed. This doesn't mean that you are not going to fail. You may even fail more than once. Everyone that has ever achieved anything in life has failed. Your self-talk will often reflect your level of self-belief, and it will also be a pretty good indicator of the probability of your success.

Get into the habit of telling yourself that you can do whatever it is that you are setting your mind to. Don't wait for this reassurance to come from outside. You need to be your own biggest cheerleader.

Here are some reasons why believing in yourself is so important:

- You can recognize your ability to achieve your goals.
- You become optimistic about the future as you set about making goals and achieving them.
- You develop the knowledge that you can achieve anything.
- You will start to treat yourself more kindly.
- You will feel uplifted and have an overall higher level of satisfaction with life.
- You will be motivated to get things done.
- You will have faith in yourself, no matter the challenges that you may be presented with.
- You will be able to recognize and appreciate the abundance around you.
- Others will be attracted to your belief in yourself and will want to know how they can achieve this too.

Tip # 7: Don't Be Afraid to Fail

Failure is an integral part of success. I realize this sounds completely counterintuitive, but it is entirely true. There has not been a single successful person in the history of the world who did not count at least one failure on their journey. Yet, we spend so much time and energy being afraid of failing. We waste time and opportunities by being fearful of what may or may not happen. It's a little crazy, isn't it? We must allow ourselves to take hold of opportunities and embrace the possibilities that lay ahead of us to overcome the inevitable failures and make it through to the successes.

If you want to avoid failing in your life, you can certainly do that. You just have to sit down and do nothing, but then know that you cannot also succeed.

This comes back to our self-talk and how you decide to phrase your failure in your internal dialogue. Is your failure going to be an opportunity to shame yourself, or will it be an opportunity to start again from a new perspective?

Tip #8: Choose Positive Thoughts More Often Than Negative Ones

I am not telling you that you will never have another negative thought again in your life. Of course you will, but you now have the tools you need to choose to overwhelm those negative thoughts with positive ones. Start choosing to swap out more and more unhelpful, negative thoughts with helpful, more positive ones.

Tip #9: Write Positive Affirmations for Yourself

As I mentioned regarding gratitude journaling, writing ideas, thoughts, and statements down can make all the difference in how real, and tangible they seem to you. The same goes for positive affirmations. I'll talk more about this in the next section because it does warrant a deeper dive. The idea is to put your positive self-talk in writing and post it wherever you spend most of your time for different activities during the day—the kitchen, bathroom, bedroom, your office, and the inside of the front door so you see it as you leave the house.

A few examples of the type of affirmations you can write include:

- *"I am brave enough to embrace all of the opportunities that present themselves to me."*
- *"I can choose how I feel today."*
- *"Today, I choose gratitude and happiness."*
- *"I am kind to myself and to others."*
- *"I have value, and I have a purpose in life."*

Tip #10: Live in the Present

Every person has things that happened in their past that could paralyze their progress if they chose to dwell on them.

Worrying about the past has absolutely no value to the present or the future, though. The only value that the past has for us is its lessons. Once those are learned, we can move on and beyond any mistakes we've made or trauma we have experienced.

If you continue to drag things from the past into the present, all you do is taint the present. This is where mindfulness really helps. Mindfulness is all about living and experiencing the here-and-now. If you feel yourself harking back to something that is long gone, bring yourself back to the present with a simple statement, "I acknowledge my past, but it has no bearing here in the present. I am here, and I am living in this moment."

Tip #11: Use Success Visualizations

Why do you think that they call some of the most successful people in the world *visionaries*? It's because they can visualize their goals and dreams before they happen. They do so in vivid detail and with conviction, pushing away any inkling of self-doubt with the mantra, "Yes, I may fail, but this is what I will receive if I succeed."

The ability to visualize your success is very closely tied to your ability to achieve it. The tangibility of a visualized goal helps to quiet the negative self-talk that would usually hold you back and carries you through the inevitable tough moments that will arise along the way.

Come up with strategies ahead of time to use when you start to feel like you can't continue. Visualize the entire journey, not just your destination. See yourself falling down and then getting back up and carrying on. Finally, picture yourself achieving the goal you have set.

Regardless of their profession, all top performers understand the importance of picturing their success in their minds before they actually do in reality. Boxing legend Muhammad Ali continuously stressed the importance of seeing himself victorious long before he undertook the actual fight. When Jim Carrey was still a struggling young actor, he imagined himself being the greatest actor in the whole world. Michael Jordan always took his last shot in his mind before he ever took one in reality. These top performers, along with many others, have mastered the technique of success visualization and openly credit it as an essential element in their success.

When you think about a big goal or dream that you want to achieve, it is normal to think about all of the obstacles that will inevitably come your way. This, in itself, is not a problem. The issue comes in when we allow these obstacles to become so enormous in our minds that it stops us from moving forward. This is when many become happy with mediocrity. Rather than creating unrealistic barriers in your mind and allowing yourself to dwell on everything that may hold you back, envision yourself victorious.

Think about what it will take to realize this visualization? What sacrifices will you need to make? How will you handle any obstacles thrown at you and still have enough energy to make it to the finish line? The key is to make your positive vision stronger and more realistic than anything that could possibly set you back.

The reality is that if you cannot picture yourself achieving a goal, the chances are that you will not achieve that goal. The more vivid you can get with your visualizations, the better it will work for you. Start thinking about your personal goals in life. Set aside time to spend at least 10 to 15 minutes picturing yourself achieving every single one.

Be sure to get as detailed as possible in your visualizations. Picture what you will do once your goal is achieved. How amazing will it feel? How will achieving this goal change the course of your life? Remember that the small details increase the likelihood of the big picture coming to fruition. It is not necessary to spend endless hours doing this. Just try to get in the habit of assembling a positive vision for your everyday life. Visualize yourself achieving success, achieving every single goal, and successfully completing every task. Notice what this does for you and how it makes you feel. This will likely become a vital part of your success arsenal.

Tip #12: Be Selective About Your Media Consumption

When you are on a journey to positive self-talk, it is easy to be derailed when it feels like the whole world is just a mass of negativity. Unfortunately, the news media is geared toward the negative. It is their job to tell the public about all the bad stuff that's happening in the world. That's fair enough, but it is your job to guard your energy. I'm not saying that you should pretend everything is fine and dandy with the world but is it necessary for you to take all of that onboard?

The timing of your news consumption is important too. If you start your day off by reading all the latest news headlines, how do you think that overload of death, destruction, and pain is going to set the tone for your day ahead? To be honest, this goes for social media too because although most people's personal profiles will only reflect the good parts of their life, by consuming social media, you are allowing an algorithm to choose what you read in your feed, and that is not always a good thing.

If your job entails that you need to stay abreast of current developments, make sure to always follow the news binge up with something positive.

You may not know this, but social media usage activates the brain's reward center by releasing dopamine. This is one of the reasons that it can become a habit and even an addiction. Part of the unhealthy cycle is that we keep coming back to social media, even though it doesn't make us feel very good in the long run. This cycle is, of course, very similar to those we experience with other addictions. We become elated when we see a like or a notification and get a dopamine hit, but the opposite happens as well.

In the same way as using a chemical drug, we think getting a fix will help, but it makes us feel worse. This comes down to an error in our ability to predict our own response. It's known as a forecasting error. We continue to think social media will make us feel good, and more often than not, it doesn't.

During a 24/7 news cycle, media exposure can increase perceptions of threat and activate our fight or flight response. This produces stress hormones like adrenaline and cortisol. Excesses of these hormones can lead to subsequent mental and physical health problems such as depression, anxiety, fatigue, and difficulty sleeping. In one study (Johnston & Davey, 1997), participants who watched just fourteen minutes of negative news showed increases in both sadness and anxiety and also showed a significant increase in the tendency to catastrophize a personal thought.

When it comes to the news, obsessing or overthinking about negative events will not help to produce any new information, but it can detrimentally affect your entire outlook on the situation. Negative obsessive thinking cyclically unearths new fears and anxieties and is associated with mental illnesses like PTSD and depression. It also affects our motivation, problem-solving abilities, and interpersonal relationships.

Tip #13: Be Helpful

Often the best way to get out of your head and remind yourself of all the things you should be grateful for is by helping others in need. This also ties into my previous tip of finding a higher purpose for yourself.

Whether you involve yourself in a structured volunteer program or simply help an old lady cross the road, being of service to others will show you how you can make a difference.

I chose an animal shelter to volunteer at because I find working with animals particularly healing, and watching a dog that I had helped nurse back to health be adopted into a new home was hugely satisfying. No matter what cause you choose, or even if you just decide to find one nice thing to do for random people each day, your confidence levels will be seriously boosted by this activity.

Studies have found that acts of kindness are linked to increased levels of wellbeing. Helping other people can also encourage us to be more active and improve our support networks. This, in turn, helps to improve our self-esteem. There is also evidence to suggest that when we help others, it promotes changes in the brain that are linked with happiness (MentalHealth.Org, n.d.). Helping others is also one of the ways that human beings create, maintain, and strengthen their social connections. For instance, volunteering and helping others can help us feel a sense of belonging, we can make new friends, and we can connect with our communities. In-person activities like volunteering at a food bank can also help reduce your own sense of loneliness and isolation.

Many people do not realize the impact that a different perspective can have on their outlook on life. We've discussed the power of different perspectives in other places in this book too. There is significant evidence that being aware of our acts of kindness and also being aware of the things we are grateful for can increase feelings of optimism, happiness, and satisfaction (MentalHealth.Org, n.d.). Doing good may help you to have a more positive outlook on your own circumstances.

Tip #14: Start Moving

Physical activity is not just beneficial for your physical health. It gives a huge boost to your mental health too. Those beautiful happy hormones that get released when you are not sitting on the couch shoving the fiftieth potato chip in your mouth are absolutely golden.

Now I am not saying you need to become a gym bunny (unless that's your thing). Instead, pick an exercise you enjoy because you will be far more likely to continue with it. Park further away from the mall entrance. Take the stairs rather than the elevator. Just move your body more. You will see the benefits.

Here are a few more easy and inexpensive ways that you can start to increase your physical activity levels:

Do Your Own Housework. Yes, I said it. Someone has to do it, so it may as well be you. One of the easiest ways to improve physical activity begins in your own home. Do your chores, regardless of whether they are indoors or outdoors.

Park Further Away From Store Entrances. Parking further away from entrances to stores or even the workplace means you will need to take more steps to reach a destination. With every step, your heart rate increases, and with continued activity, overall health improves. This has the same effect as walking on a treadmill or engaging in any other exercise.

Get off the Bus/Subway/Taxi a Few Blocks Early. While this may not be possible for those that drive themselves to work or the store, you still have the option to park a few blocks away. This is another excellent idea for walking more and follows the benefits noted by parking further away from entrances too.

Dance With the Music. Yes, dancing is exercise too. It stimulates the cells of the body, and over time, your endurance increases too. Also, listening to music while walking helps to pass the time and encourages you to continue longer than you might have if you weren't listening to music.

Invest in a Standing Desk. Sitting for long periods of time is associated with a wide range of health problems. Instead of sitting down for too long, consider standing while you are working at the computer or desk. A converting sit-to-standing desk allows you to sit and rest when necessary.

Make Use of Apps That Encourage Physical Activity. There are thousands of apps available that promote an active lifestyle. Such apps can help remind you to get up and move around and also measure your activity for the day so that you can set goals and improve.

Walk instead of driving where possible. If your neighborhood is safe to do so, walk to the store. Walk your kids to school. If a drive in the car takes five minutes or less, you really can walk that. Get into the habit of walking after a family dinner too. A Sunday walk can even replace a Sunday drive.

Set Step Goals. This can be for your usual steps during your day. Once you start measuring, you'll be amazed at how quickly they add up. Start out by measuring your normal step count without putting any additional effort in. That becomes your threshold, and you can set your goals from there. If you get home and your step goal has not been achieved, you will be motivated to make those steps up before settling in for the night.

Tip #15: Set Goals and Dream Big

An excellent way to encourage positive self-talk is to set goals and have dreams that you can start working toward. Dream as big as you like, but be sure to break down the biggest goals into small manageable chunks.

A dream is a clear vision of what you want for your future. It is a detailed multi-dimensional picture including details such as where you are living, how you are spending your days, how much money you have funding your dream, who you are sharing your dream with, and so forth. You can even deepen the goal by bringing in other senses than sight. What does your dream smell like? Envisioning your future does not come naturally for most people. You will need to practice to be able to visualize what you want.

Decide where you want to be in 5, 10, or 15 years and then work out what you need to do along the way to get there. Celebrate every single small goal you achieve because it's paving the way to the bigger goal. By celebrating these small wins, you will become more and more assured of your abilities, and your self-confidence will grow each time.

Allow yourself the flexibility to sometimes stumble and to shift your direction if you need to. As long as you are working toward a goal, it doesn't matter how you get there.

The Power of Affirmations

We briefly touched on positive affirmations in the previous sections, and I have found them to be so powerful that I need to go deeper into this here. Upfront, I want you to know that this is not just some whimsical idea. The power of positive affirmations is based on science.

So, what are positive affirmations? They are very simply positive statements or phrases that challenge negative and unhelpful thinking. Using positive affirmations in your life can be easy. All you need to do is select a phrase that has deep meaning and repeat it to yourself. Positive affirmations can also be used as motivation and to boost self-esteem.

The Science Behind Positive Affirmations

There is a key psychological theory that backs up the use of positive affirmations. It is called Self-Affirmation Theory (Moore, 2019). This theory has three main ideas that form its foundation.

The first is that by using self-affirmation, human beings can keep up a global narrative about themselves. This narrative or story is that we are moral, flexible, and adaptive. This narrative forms part of our self-identity. I must point out that self-identity is not the same as having a fixed concept of ourselves that comes with labels like "wife," "son," " sister, or "mother." Self-identity allows us to be more flexible about how we see ourselves and, as a result, how we see our success. This means that we can also choose to see the positive aspects of ourselves rather than just the negative aspects.

The second part of Self-Affirmation Theory is the idea that self-identity is not about being perfect or exceptional. Instead, it is about being good at the things we value.

The final aspect of the Self-Affirmation Theory is that we act in ways that earn us recognition for the things that we value. We don't say something like, "I am a strong and capable person" so that we can receive praise for it; we do so because we want to earn recognition for behaving in ways that warrant the statement.

So that's the theory that backs up positive affirmations, but is there physical evidence that backs it up?

The development of this theory led the neuroscience community to wonder whether there would be measurable brain activity to prove the effects of positive affirmations. MRIs (brain scans) of people practicing self-affirming tasks like repeating positive affirmations show that neural pathways are developed when this is done. It has a physical impact on the brain (Moore, 2019). Neural pathways are, of course, strengthened the more you do something, so by repeating positive affirmations regularly, we can build new pathways in our brain. This research would also show that by developing these new neural pathways, we are better able to logically assess and analyze information about ourselves (Moore, 2019). In our context, this means that we get better at throwing out negative self-talk and accepting positive self-talk.

The Benefits of Daily Positive Affirmations

Some of the studies (Moore, 2019) carried out to measure the value of positive affirmations have also led to the realization that there are a number of calculable benefits from the practice. These include:

- A decrease in stress which negatively impacts health.

- A boost in physical activity is a direct result of affirmations.
- A change in the way we view otherwise "threatening" messages such as criticism and interventions.
- We are less likely to ignore information about a negative impact on our health, and we are more likely to undertake actions that improve our health.
- Academic performance is improved.

- Stress and negative repetitive thoughts are reduced.
- Levels of mental and physical resilience increase.
- An optimistic mindset is formed, which has its own benefits, including dealing with negative experiences better and being less likely to linger on negativity.

Examples of Positive Affirmations

While it is really important that you choose affirmations that mean something to you personally, there are many examples that you can start to build off. You will find that some work well for your personal situation and that others need to be adapted.

"All is well."
"I am capable and confident."
"I only allow positive people into my life.
"I am enough."
"I am constantly surrounded by positive energy."

"I am choosing to be mindful and present at this moment."
"I feel ever-multiplying gratitude for my life.
"I am choosing to use affirmations that serve my higher self."
"I always fulfill the promises I make to others and myself."
"I use every opportunity to share happiness with others."
"I am alive and filled with energy."
"I control how I respond to the behavior of other people."
"I can forgive and let go."
"I take in positivity and let go of negativity."
"I am creative, talented, and successful."
"I become stronger every day."
"I only speak to myself with kindness."
"My life is playing out exactly as it is meant to."

Making A Habit Out of Journaling

I have presented journaling as an excellent tool for working against toxic thinking in several places in this book. It is a phenomenal way to put what is happening in our heads in black and white so that we can see it and not just experience it.

Journaling helps us to filter out, analyze, and deeply understand the habits that our mind develops. It also helps us unearth deeply embedded thoughts, distortions, and biases that we may otherwise be unaware of. Journaling became a huge part of my own journey out of toxic thinking. When I started to see my thoughts in words on paper, I understood what was really going on in my head. This powerful impact on my life caused me to make journaling a habit and use it to this day, to get out of my head and break the vicious circles that so often form subconsciously.

By practicing journaling as a habit, you will reduce the impact that negative self-talk has on you and, essentially, use it against itself. You will be able to boost your self-esteem and confidence levels considerably.

Journaling Prompts

I really would like you to give journaling a try. It is life-changing and, in our context, one of the most powerful tools against negative self-talk. You can journal however you like. You can use a handwritten journal or an electronic one. I find that there is something deeply personal and connecting about using a handwritten journal. It just makes the experience more powerful somehow.

When you journal, you tap into deeper parts of yourself. You become clearer about who you are and what you want out of life. By journaling, you are essentially working on your relationship with yourself. It is, after all, the most important relationship you will ever have.

Journaling can be done in different ways. You can journal about your day and see what you come up with, or you can journal around a specific prompt. It often helps beginners to have prompts to start off with, but as you get more proficient at journaling, you will probably find that you no longer need them. Your mind will begin to guide you into what you need to journal about that day.

Journaling Prompts for Reflecting On Your Day

- Can you think of five things that went well today?
- What happened today that was challenging and what lessons did you take from your response to that challenge?
- What made you happy today? Be as specific as you can.
- What are ten things or people that you are grateful for today?
- What would you want tomorrow to be like?

Journaling Prompts for Reflecting On Your Week

- Which people made you feel good this week? How did they do that?
- What is the one thing you regret about this week, and what did you learn from that mistake?
- What did you do this week that pleasantly surprised you? Was there something you did or achieved that the old you wouldn't have been able to?

- In which ways were you able to move closer to your goals this week?
- Is there anything you would have done differently this week?
- What activities did you enjoy this week?
- What did you learn?

Journaling Prompts to Improve Self-Esteem

- What positive aspects of yourself make you unique?
- Write a letter to your body expressing your gratitude for all of the amazing things it does.
- What would you like to be remembered for, and what do you need to achieve in order to be remembered this way?
- List all the things you would like to achieve before next year.
- List all of the best traits of your character.
- Starting as far back in your life as you can remember, list all of the things you've achieved.
- What things are you particularly good at?
- If your best friend were writing in your journal, how would they describe you?
- If you were assured that you would not fail, what would you try?
- Who are some of the people you count as role models, and how can you be more like those people?

- What would you be doing with your time if money was not a consideration?
- If you could become an expert in any topic, which would it be?
- Think about a person that is toxic in your life. Write down and describe in detail the types of feelings they evoke in you. Now write down how it would feel to release those feelings and no longer have them as part of you.
- Pretend that you are writing the acknowledgments page in the book of your life.
- What would the person that you were in high school love about who you are right now?

"A negative mind will never give you a positive life."

— ZIAD K. ABDELNOUR

CONCLUSION

In *Toxic Thinking,* I have passed on the research, information, and tips that helped me to move past my toxic thinking trap.

So many of us go through our whole lives without really knowing how deeply our inner voice affects us. The voice within us develops pretty early on in our lives, and as we go through different things, it can either become a help or a hindrance as we've learned. The choice is ours. In order to harness the power of our inner critic, we need to understand whether it is helpful or harmful and how to shift it from critic to cheerleader.

Until I started to delve down into negative self-talk, I did not realize how deeply it had affected my life, and I have no doubt that you will be surprised on your journey too. We often mistake the things we do or say as being part of our character or personality when they aren't—they are entrenched habits that we've developed due to negative-self talk. Once we come to this realization, we can start to return to our true selves.

There are many different types of negative self-talk, and we must become intimately familiar with the different types so that we can identify them in ourselves. You will likely identify more of one type of negative self-talk in yourself than another simply because we are all unique, and so are the experiences we've had.

I found that certain parts of CBT and other forms of therapy like ACT were highly beneficial in this journey, which is why I have included cognitive defusion and cognitive restructuring in this book. They are vital parts of the process, and I highly recommend that you read and reread those sections as many times as you need to in order to fully understand the techniques. Your negative self-talk cycle did not form overnight, and by the same token, it will take some time to start breaking it down. With commitment and practice, though, I can guarantee you that it's possible.

The cognitive defusion process will help you separate yourself from the narrative that has formed around your negative self-talk. It will allow you to see yourself as you are and not how your self-talk paints you. Cognitive restructuring will help to find a new narrative, one that is more logical and accurate, so that you can move forward with a healthier and more realistic picture of who you are and what you are capable of.

The final stage of our process involves building yourself back up again. You will need to find that place inside you where your confidence and positivity live and feed it so that it grows. This is perhaps the most significant impact that negative self-talk has on us—our confidence is sometimes completely decimated. That causes a massive number of other issues in turn.

Positive self-talk is just as powerful as negative self-talk, only it is helpful rather than harmful, and just as we subconsciously learned to allow negative self-talk to fester in our minds, we can teach ourselves to choose positive self-talk as well. Same process, different outcome. I provided you with 15 tips to help you grow your confidence and start using positive self-talk rather than its negative counterpart. Not all of these tips will work for you, but many will. Try them and figure out which works best for your personal circumstances.

I've focused on specific techniques that I found to work well in this book, and journaling is one of those. I would like to think that you will try every technique in this book at least once, but if you choose only one to start right away, let it be journaling. I cannot tell you how this simple practice has changed my life, and I know that it will do the same for you.

When I started to recover from my toxic thinking, I never imagined that I would one day pen this book. When you start to see the world from a different perspective and witness the phenomenal changes in your life, it's difficult not to share it. Although I am well aware that the techniques that worked for me will not work for everyone, I do know that the suggestions will assist many people in this book. The thing about correcting your self-talk is that it's not just you that benefits. When you live your life from a more positive perspective, everyone around you benefits. If you are a parent, your children will most definitely benefit from you being able to cast aside unhelpful negative self-talk. After all, your self-talk is helping to shape theirs.

Changing the way you interact with yourself internally, though, will have even more far-reaching effects. Every person you come into contact with will be touched in some way by your positivity. Most importantly, your own life will be transformed.

In the techniques you have learned on these pages, you have learned how to identify negative self-talk and how to overcome it. You now understand how to convert toxic thinking into positive interactions with yourself. When we live our lives with a positive outlook, we can live a better life from a mental, emotional, and physical perspective. You now have a practical approach to help you cut back on negative self-talk.

Having come back from a pretty dark place myself, it pains me to think that there are people that will never pull themselves out of toxic thinking. I am glad, however, that each person that reads this book will have the opportunity to overcome this painful cycle. If you have gained value from this book, please review and share it on Amazon and recommend it to those that you think will also gain benefit from it. In this way, we can start spreading positivity and having more and more people kicking toxic thinking to the curb.

You are at the very beginning of a challenging but exciting journey. You are about to take back your life and start to live the way you deserve. No longer will you be held back by the chains of negative self-talk. You have the tools to break the shackles, and now it's up to you to do it.

REFERENCES

Colier, N. (2019, April 15). Negative Thinking: A Dangerous Addiction. Psychology Today. https://www.psychologytoday.com/us/blog/inviting-monkey-tea/201904/negative-thinking-dangerous-addiction

Hampton, D. (2018, July 22). 10 Common Negative Thinking Patterns and How You Can Change Them. The Best Brain Possible. https://thebestbrainpossible.com/negative-thinking-depression-mind/

Itani, O. (2020, July 7). How to Silence Your Inner Critic and Amplify Your Confidence. https://www.omaritani.com/blog/how-to-silence-your-inner-critic

Johnston, W. M., & Davey, G. C. L. (1997). The psychological impact of negative TV news bulletins: The catastrophizing of personal worries. British Journal of Psychology, 88(1), 85–91. https://doi.org/10.1111/j.2044-8295.1997.tb02622.x

Mead, E. (2019, September 26). What is Positive Self-Talk? (Incl. Examples). PositivePsychology.com. https://positivepsychology.com/positive-self-talk/

MentalHealth.org. (n.d.). Kindness Matters Guide. Mental Health. Org UK. https://www.mentalhealth.org.uk/campaigns/kindness/kindness-matters-guide

Norris, W. (2018, December 6). Some thoughts on thoughts: The inner critic and self-talk. Counseling Today. https://ct.counseling.org/2018/12/some-thoughts-on-thoughts-the-inner-critic-and-self -talk/

Powell, A. (2018, April 9). Harvard researchers study how mindfulness may change the brain in depressed patients. Harvard Gazette; https://news.harvard.edu/gazette/story/2018/04/harvard-researchers-study-how-mindfulness-may-change-the-brain-in-depressed-patients/

Raypole, C. (2019, November 21). How to Deal With Toxic People: 17 Tips. Healthline. https://www.healthline.com/health/how-to-deal-with-toxic-people

Ribeiro, M. (2019, July 4). How to Become Mentally Strong: 14 Strategies for Building Resilience. PositivePsychology.com. https://positivepsychology.com/mentally-strong/

Scott, E. (2020, February 25). How to Reduce Negative Self-Talk for a Better Life. Verywell Mind. https://www.verywellmind.com/negative-self-talk-and-how-it-affects-us-4161304

Simone, F. (2017, December 4). Negative Self-Talk: Don't Let It Overwhelm You.Psychology Today. https://www.psychologytoday.com/us/blog/family-affair/201712/negative-self-talk-dont-let-it-overwhelm-you

Shukla, A. (2019, September 26). Stop/Control Negative Thoughts With Cognitive Defusion & Cognitive Restructuring Techniques. Cognition Today. https://cognitiontoday.com/stop-negative-thoughts-with-cognitive-defusion-cognitive-restructuring-techniques/#What_is_Cognitive_Defusion

Shukla, A. (2018, June 12). How to remain calm: reducing stress, anxiousness, and social anxiety. Cognition Today. https://cognitiontoday.com/how-to-remain-calm-reducing-stress-anxiousness-and-social-anxiety/

Stephens, C. (2019, January 8). The 5-Minute Technique I Use to Defeat Negative Self-Talk. Healthline. https://www.healthline.com/health/mental-health/self-talk-exercises#How-to-use-the-5-minute-triple-column-technique-

Underwood, A. (2018, May 2). Metaphors. What Is a Metaphor? —Definition and Examples | Grammarly. https://www.grammarly.com/blog/metaphor/

Wikipedia Contributors. (2019, November 19). Private speech. Wikipedia; Wikimedia Foundation. https://en.wikipedia.org/wiki/Private_speech

Wikipedia Contributors. (2019a, September 30). Socratic questioning. Wikipedia; Wikimedia Foundation. https://en.wikipedia.org/wiki/Socratic_questioning

CPSIA information can be obtained
at www.ICGtesting.com
Printed in the USA
LVHW110146280323
742726LV00009B/526

9 781399 902496